# Geography Matters 3

## HIGHER

**Series Editor:**

John Hopkin

**Authors:**

Nicola Arber, Bournville School, Birmingham

Rob Bowden, Development Education Centre, Birmingham

Lisa James, Cockshut Hill School, Birmingham

Sue Lomas, Henbury High School, Macclesfield

Garrett Nagle, St Edward's School, Oxford

Roger Sanders, Sir John Talbot's School, Whitchurch

Linda Thompson, formerly at Sandbach School, Sandbach

Paul Thompson, Ounsdale High School, Wolverhampton

Heinemann Educational Publishers
Halley Court, Jordan Hill, Oxford, OX2 8EJ
a division of Reed Educational & Professional Publishing Ltd
Heinemann is a registered trademark of Reed Educational & Professional Publishing Ltd

OXFORD MELBOURNE AUCKLAND
JOHANNESBURG BLANTYRE GABORONE
IBADAN PORTSMOUTH NH (USA) CHICAGO

© Nicola Arber, Rob Bowden, Lisa James, Sue Lomas, Garrett Nagle, Roger Sanders, Linda Thompson, Paul Thompson, 2002

First published 2002

ISBN 0 435 35526 0

06 05 04 03 02
10 9 8 7 6 5 4 3 2

Designed and illustrated by Gecko Ltd, Bicester, Oxon, Tokay, Roger Penwill, John Storey, and Geoff Ward
Original illustrations © Heinemann Educational Publishers 2001
Printed and bound in Spain by Edelvives

**Acknowledgements**
The authors and publishers would like to thank the following for permission to reproduce copyright: material.

**Photos**
**p. 4** *A* Panos Pictures/A. le Garsmeur, *B* Panos Pictures/Rob Cousins, *C* Robert Harding/Doug Traverso, *D*: Popperfoto/Reuters/Rafiqur Rahman, *E*: Science Photo Library/Ted Kerasote; **p. 5** *F* Woodfall Wild Images/Nigel Hicks, *G* Robert Harding/C. Bowman, *H* Hutchison Library/Ian Lloyd; **p. 6** *top:* Flying Colours *bottom*: Hutchison Library/Crispin Hughes; **p. 7** Still Pictures/David Drain; **p. 8** *A*: Panos Pictures/Betty Press, *B*: Robert Harding/Brian Harrison; **p. 10** Panos Pictures/Jon Spaull; **p. 15** Rob Bowden; **p. 16** Rob Bowden; **p.18** Panos Pictures/Jeremy Hartley; **p. 20** *A* Science Photo Library/Ted Kerasote, *B*: Robert Harding Picture Library; **p. 22** *A* Robert Harding/Explorer, *B*: Still Pictures, *C*: Spectrum Colour Library; **p. 24** *A*: Still Pictures/Pierre Gleizes, *B*: World Pictures, *C*: Spectrum Colour Library/P. Thompson; **p. 25** *D*: World Pictures, *E* Robert Harding Picture Library/S. Harris, *F* Robert Harding Picture Library/C. Martin; **p. 26** *A* Still Pictures/Patrick Bertrand, *B* Magnum Photos/Gilles Peress, *C* Spectrum Colour Library; **p. 28** *B* Still Pictures/Klein/Hubert, *A* Robert Harding Picture Library; **p. 30** Spectrum Colour Library; **p. 34** Woodfall Wild Images/Bob Gibbons; **p. 35** Environmental Images/Oliver Waterlow; **p. 36** *C*: Science Photo Library, *D:* Still Pictures/J.F. Mutzig, *E*: Still Pictures/Pierre Gleizes; **p. 37** Oxford Scientific Films/Raymond Blythe; **p. 38** Robert Harding Picture Library/E. Simanor; **p. 40** Corbis; **p. 44** Advertising Archives; **p. 45** *B*: Associated Press/Richard Vogel, *C*: Popperfoto/Paolo Cocco/Reuters; **p. 52** Nike; **p. 60** *A* Still Pictures/Mark Edwards, *B* Spectrum Colour Library, *C*: Hutchison Picture Library/Nigel Sitwell, *D* Spectrum Colour Library, *E*: World Pictures, *F*: Spectrum Colour Library; *G*: Spectrum Colour Library, **p. 64** Skyscan; **p. 66** World Pictures; **p. 73** *top R*: Science Photo Library/Worldsat International and J. Knighton, *middle L*: Science Photo Library/Julian Baum & David Angus; **p. 74** Eye Ubiquitous/Paul Thompson; **p. 75** Robert Harding Picture Library/Adam Woolfitt; **p. 76** *A*: Spectrum Colour Library, *B*: The Art Archive/Musée Guimet Paris/Dagli Orti; **p. 78** *B* Robert Harding Picture Library/Tony Waltham, *C*: Robert Harding Picture Library/Gina Corrigan, *D*: Picture Works/Ingrid Booz Morejohn; **p. 79** *E* Associated Press/Greg Baker, *F*: Associated Press/Zhou Wenguang, **p. 81** Spectrum Colour Library; **p. 82** *top R*: Robert Harding Picture Library/Gavin Hellier, *top L*: Spectrum Colour Library, *bottom*: Corbis/Steve Kaufmal; **p. 83** *top R*: Magnum Photos, Still Pictures/Francois Suchel; **p. 85** *top L*: Rex Features/IWASA, *middle R*: Associated Press/David Guttenfelder, *bottom L*: Science Photo Library/NASA; **p. 87** *top L*: Robert Harding Picture Library/Chester Beatty Library, *middle R*: James Davis Travel Photography, *bottom R*: Eye Ubiquitous/Frank Leather; **p. 88** Associated Press/Zxinhua; **p. 89** Picture Works/Ingrid Booz Morejohn; **p. 90** Mitsubishi Electric Europe; **p. 91** Spectacular China; **p. 92** *C*: & **p. 70** *C* Eye Ubiquitous/Nick Bonetti; **p. 92** *D*: & **p. 70** *D*: Eye Ubiquitous/Chris Fairclough; **p. 92** *E*: & **p. 71** *F* Spectrum Colour Library; **p. 92** *F*: & **p. 71** *E*: Robert Harding Picture Library/Nigel Blythe; **p. 92** *G*: & **p. 71** *G*: Robert Harding Picture Library; **p. 92** *H* and **p. 71** *H* Still Pictures/Hartmut Schwarzbach; **p. 94** Dr Jurg Alean/Stromboli; **p. 97** *top*: Spectrum Colour Library, *bottom*: Corbis/Mike Zens; **p. 99** *L*: Popperfoto/Reuters, *R*: Rex Features/Sipa Press; **p. 102** Dr Jurg Alean/Stromboli; **p. 103** Science Photo Library/David Parker; **p. 106** *L*: Earthquake Hazard Centre/Rajendra Desai, *R*: Hutchison Picture Library/Bernard Regent; **p. 108** *middle L*: Rex Features/Nils Jorgensen, *middle R*: AP Photos/Findlay Kember, *bottom L*: Still Pictures/Klaus Andrews; **p. 110** *top L*: Getmapping.com, *bottom L*: BMW AG; **p. 112** author; **p. 113** *middle R*: Chris Honeywell, *top R*: Garett Nagle; **p. 114** *middle R*: BMW AG, *bottom L*: BMW AG; **p. 115** BMW AG; **p. 118** Get Mapping; **p. 120** author; **p. 123** author; **p. 128** Science Photo Library/Dr. Jeremy Burgess; **p. 129** *top R*: Still Pictures/Fred Dott; *top L*: Environmental Images/S. Mahoney; **p. 130** *A*: Science Photo Library/Microfield Scientific Ltd., *B*: Still Pictures/Roland Birke, *C*: Oxford Scientific Films/Paul Kay, *D*: Oxford Scientific Films/Sue Scott, *E*: Still Pictures/J.P. Sylvestre, *F*: Woodfall Wild Images/Mark Hamblin, *G:* Woodfall Wild Images/Tom Campbell, *H*: Woodfall Wild Images/Bill Coster, *I*: Science Photo Library/Rudiger Lehnan; **p. 134** Axiom/Jonathan Renouf; **p. 135** *middle R*: Greenpeace, *bottom R*: Science Photo Library/Tom McHugh; **p. 136** *F*: Still Pictures/Klaus Andrews, *F* Robert Harding Picture Library, *G*: Science Photo Library/NASA; **p. 137** Science Photo Library/Simon Fraser, *J* Environmental Images/Martin Bond, *top R*: Still Pictures/Hartmut Schwarzbach; **p. 138** Greenpeace; **p. 139** *O*: Oxford Scientific Films/Colin Monteath, *P*: Panos Pictures/Fred Hoogervorst.

**Text, Maps and Diagrams**
**p. 6 Source D** ActionAid *Fighting Poverty Together*, ActionAid's Strategy 1999–2003; **p. 77 Source C** (1/12/2000, 20/5/2001) *The Daily Telegraph* **p. 6 Source B** DFID, *Eliminating World Poverty: A Challenge for the 21ˢᵗ century: a summary* 1997; **p. 56** DFID, *Making globalisation work for the world's poor: an introduction to the UK Government's White Paper on International Development 2000*; **p. 20 Source C** Forestry Stewardship Council A.C; **p. 50 Source E** (Andrew Osborne 23/11/2000) *The Guardian* **p. 63 Source E** *The Guardian* web site; **p. 77 Source C** (3/4/2001, 15/5/2001, 13/6/2001) *The Guardian*; **p. 65 Source F, 112, Sources A, B, 119** Maps reproduced from Ordinance Survey mapping with the permission of the Controller of Her Majesty's Stationery Office, ©Crown Copyright. All rights reserved. Licence No. 10000230; **p. 77 Source C** (12/9/2000, 5/4/2001) *The Times*; **p. 6 Source A, 9 Source C**, United Nations Development Programme, *Human Development Report* 1999; **p.12 Source B, 81 Source B** United Nations Human Development Index 1998; **p.14 Source A, 17 Source B, 56 Sources A, B** United Nations Development Programme 1999; **p. 17 Source C** United Nations Development Programme 2000; **p. 17 Source C** 1996) UNICEF; **p. 7 Source A** *Western Mail*; **p. 68 Source A** (Spring 1999) *Which* Magazines; **p. 6 Source C** World Bank *World Development Report* 1999, **p. 12 Source A** (1998) World Bank; **p. 20 Source D** World Commission on Environment and Development *Our Common Future* 1987.

*Throughout the book these symbols are used with activities that use literacy, numeracy and ICT skills.*

# Contents

**Websites** The authors have provided a list of topic-linked websites for the use alongside *Geography Matters 3, Higher* which can be found at www.heinemann.co.uk/hotlinks. Please insert the code GM3PH at the website to access them.

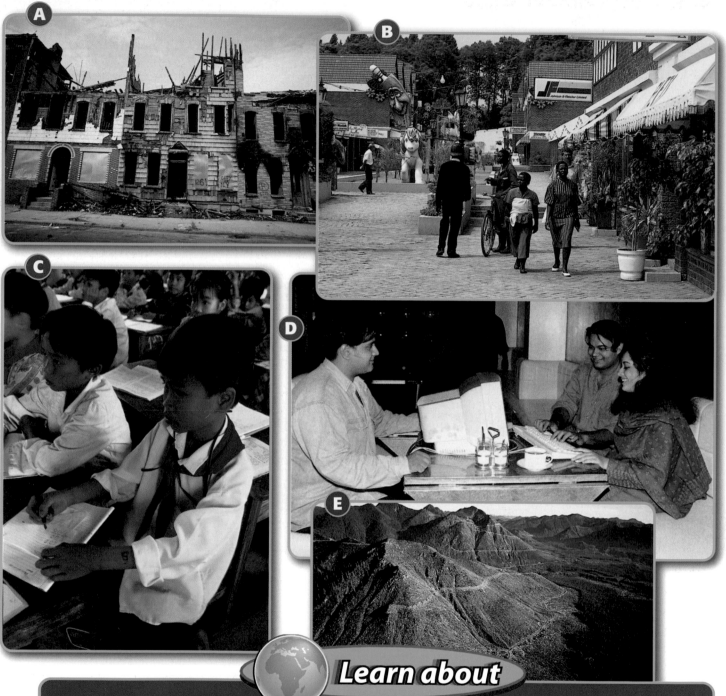

A

B

C

D

E

## Learn about

Development affects us all, but in very different ways. For some it can bring great benefits, such as better jobs or improved health, but for others it brings little change in their day-to-day lives and may even make things worse. In this unit you will explore what development means and you will learn:

◉ what development means to different people

◉ what development means in your local area

◉ how patterns of development vary globally

◉ how different parts of the world are connected by development

◉ how geographers analyse data to understand development

◉ who benefits and who loses as a result of development

◉ what 'sustainable development' means

◉ what governments and others do to help development.

# Perceptions of development

## Getting Technical ▼

⑤ **Perception:** the way we experience and interpret (perceive) the world around us. If someone smiles, your perception might be that they are happy. Perception is important to geographers because different people can perceive the same place or event in different ways.

⑤ **MEDCs** (More Economically Developed Countries): wealthy and industrialised nations. They include those from North America and Western Europe and Australia, New Zealand and Japan. They are also known as *Industrialised Countries*, *Developed Countries*, *The North* or *The First World*.

⑤ **LEDCs** (Less Economically Developed Countries): usually poorer and more agricultural nations. Many of these countries are in Central and South America, Africa and Asia. They are also known as *Developing Countries*, *The South* or *The Third World*.

## Activities

### Discussion activity

1. Working in a small group, study the photographs on these pages.

   a Decide which images represent 'more developed' places (MEDCs) and which represent 'less developed' places (LEDCs). Write down the reasons behind your decisions.

   b For each photograph, try to agree on at least two things it tells you about development. Try not to repeat your ideas.

2. Compare your ideas with those of other groups. Make a note of any differences or similarities and discuss your differing perceptions.

3. Using your responses to **1** and **2**, work as a class to try to write a definition of development. Begin with 'Development is ...'.

4. Start a word bank for this unit with the key words you have used so far. 📖

5

People think about development in many different ways. Their viewpoints will depend on their own situations and experiences of development. Think about these differing definitions and views of development.

*The real wealth of a nation is its people. And the purpose of development is to create an environment for people to enjoy long, healthy and creative lives.*

**A** United Nations Development Programme (from *Human Development Report*, 1999)

We shall refocus our international development efforts to eliminate poverty. We shall support policies which create sustainable livelihoods for poor people, promote human development and conserve the environment.

*Clare Short MP*

**B** UK Department For International Development (from *Eliminating World Poverty* – Summary, 1997)

Raising incomes is only one among many development objectives. Improving quality of life involves better health services and educational opportunities, greater participation in public life, a clean environment, equity and more.

**C** World Bank (from *World Development Report*, 1999)

Poverty and the denial of basic needs (such as education, information and security) is a violation of fundamental human rights. The causes of poverty are very much rooted in the unjust distribution of resources. Eradicating poverty without understanding inequality will not yield lasting solutions.

**D** ActionAid (from *Fighting Poverty Together: ActionAid's Strategy 1999–2003*)

Development for me is being able to educate my children and keep them healthy so that they have greater opportunities to earn money and have a better life than me.

**E** Fisherman, Lake Victoria, Uganda, 1999

## Activities

**1 a** Look at opinions **A** to **E** above. In a group, pick out the key words used to describe development. Write them in a grid like the one here, recording the key word, and the definitions it appears in. The first one has been done for you.

| Key word | Definitions | Frequency |
|----------|-------------|-----------|
| Poverty | B, D | 3 |
| | | |

**b** Read again the definition of development your class wrote for activity **3** on page 5. Calling this definition **F**, add its key words to your table.

**c** Now fill in the frequency of each key word you have identified.

**2 a** Working in a pair or small group, use the five most frequent key words to help write your own definition of development. Compare your definition with those of other groups; have your ideas changed?

**b** If your views have changed from classroom definition **F**, discuss what might have caused the changes. What does this tell you about definitions and views of development?

**3** Add any new words to your word bank for this unit.

**4** **Extension**

Write an acrostic poem like the one here to show what you understand by the word DEVELOPMENT.

D................................
E................................
V................................

Development is not just about global changes and the well-being of whole countries – it involves your own neighbourhood too. In some cases development can happen indirectly through connections between where you live and far-off places. Sometimes development can affect your neighbourhood more directly – for example, there may be plans to build a new road or to close a nearby mine or factory. The newspaper cuttings in **B** are about the development of wind farms in Mid Wales.

### £11m wind farm project breezes in

The start of a £11m wind farm project in Mid Wales will provide power for 7000 homes. The managing director of National Wind Power said: 'It will mean a further input of work to the local community and at the same time make a large and positive contribution to the environment.'

### Blowing away wind farm myths

… electricity made using coal contributes to global warming and to acid rain, which continues to cause widespread damage throughout Wales. Wind energy, on the other hand, is pollution-free.

## Mind blowing

A good night's sleep is just a dream for inhabitants of a once delightful rural Welsh village. The constant drone of twenty new turbines is driving them to distraction. Windmills, they say, have ruined their lives.

### Plea for balance in wind farm debate

Wind farms are generally highly visible, and they are sometimes more noisy than they should be. But they are the most energy-efficient of all the electricity generating technologies.

" Wind farm power is unreliable. Wind farms with their tiny and unreliable power production can never replace power stations. "

### Turbine energy is just hot air

… each windmill, put up at a cost of £500 000, will produce no more than 0.00035 per cent of the total UK power requirement.

Four giant turbines at Wales's first commercial wind farm were wrecked when gale force winds ripped across the Welsh hilltop site.

'These awful things could destroy the beauty and quietness of the Welsh countryside when it's covered in these dreadful propellors.'

'Our house is unsellable.'

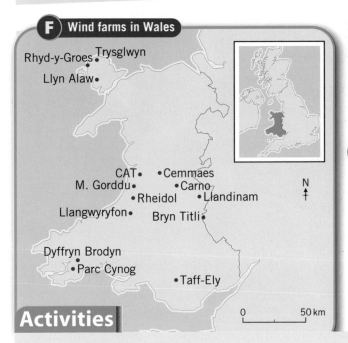

**F** Wind farms in Wales

Rhyd-y-Groes •
Trysglwyn •
Llyn Alaw •

CAT •
M. Gorddu •
• Cemmaes
• Carno
• Rheidol • Llandinam
Llangwyryfon • Bryn Titli •

Dyffryn Brodyn
• Parc Cynog
• Taff-Ely

N

0        50 km

**G** Views on wind farm development taken from the *Western Mail*

**H** A wind farm at Llandinam, Wales

## Activities

1. Draw two spider diagrams, one to show who will benefit from this wind farm development (the winners) and one to show who will suffer (the losers). Work with a partner or in a small group to add as many connections to the diagrams as you can think of.

2. Colour code your diagrams in two colours to show who is affected directly and who is more indirectly affected. Remember to add a key.

3. Using local newspapers or the Internet, research development projects in your own community. Make a list of what the main issues are and repeat activities **1** and **2**. If there are several issues, divide into groups and take one each.

4. Are there similarities and differences between your local development issues and the development issues in Mid Wales?

# Development and quality of life

**A** Village on Lake Volta, Ghana

**B** Rush hour on London Bridge

The quality of life enjoyed by individuals depends greatly on whether they live in a more or less developed country. In the UK, for example, a child born today can expect to live for around 77 years, to attend school and to have enough food to eat. But a child born today in Kenya can expect to live to just 52, has only a 68 per cent chance of completing primary school and a 59 per cent chance of regularly getting enough food to eat. People living in more developed countries generally enjoy a better quality of life than people in less developed countries, as shown in table **C**.

## Getting Technical ▾

⊚ **Standard of living** is used to describe the economic well-being of people. Those with greater wealth are assumed to have a higher standard of living than those with less money. Using this measure, a higher standard of living is achieved by economic growth.

⊚ **Quality of life** considers the way in which people live their daily lives, not just how poor or wealthy they are. Do they have enough to eat? Can they afford to educate their children? Do they have shelter at night? These types of questions are asked in order to measure quality of life.

| Region of the world | Life expectancy (years) | Under-five mortality rate (per thousand) | Adult literacy rate (%) (US $) | GNP per capita |
|---|---|---|---|---|
| Sub-Saharan Africa | 49 | 172 | 58.5 | 530 |
| Arab States | 66 | 72 | 59.7 | 2 200 |
| East Asia | 70 | 46 | 83.4 | 1 140 |
| South-East Asia | 66 | 57 | 88.2 | 1 130 |
| South Asia | 63 | 106 | 54.3 | 490 |
| Latin America and the Caribbean | 69 | 39 | 87.7 | 3 830 |
| Eastern Europe and former USSR | 69 | 33 | 98.6 | 2 100 |
| Industrialised countries | 76 | 14 | 97.4 | 20 900 |
| World | 67 | 84 | 78.8 | 4 910 |

*Data taken from UNDP Human Development Report 2000*

**C** Key variations in quality of life by region, 1998

## Activities

1. Study photographs **A** and **B** carefully and locate them using an atlas.

2. Draw a Development Compass Rose (DCR) as shown in **D** in the centre of a large sheet of paper.

3. Using the DCR, work in a group to analyse the two photographs and record your ideas on your sheet of paper. Look for clues that show what types of changes might be happening and who is making the decisions. Are the changes Natural, Economic or Social? Remember that they could be a combination of these.

4. Compare your analysis of the two photographs. Look for issues and questions that are (i) similar and (ii) different. Copy your answers into a table like the one below.

|  | Similarities | Differences |
|---|---|---|
| Natural – environment |  |  |
| Economic |  |  |
| Social |  |  |
| Who Decides? Political |  |  |

5. **Extension**

   Using your work on these two photos, think what a typical day might be like for people living in the locations shown in **A** and **B**. Write a diary entry for someone in each location.

**help!**

- You may want to use a separate sheet for each photograph, or a different colour pen to show the differences.

- Remember that some of the issues might apply to both photographs.

**D** Development Compass Rose

**Natural**
These are actions or decisions that bring about changes in the physical environment

**Who decides?**
These are the people or organisations who make decisions or take actions that bring about changes

**Economic**
These are actions or decisions that in some way involve money

**Social**
These are actions or decisions that affect people and the way they live their daily lives

# Regional variations in development

Differences in quality of life can also be found *within* countries – people in more and less developed countries can sometimes share a similar quality of life. For example, homeless people living in the UK may have much in common with people in less developed countries. Similarly, wealthy business owners or managers living in Kenya may enjoy a quality of life as good as that of people living in more developed countries, or even better. Geographers call these differences **inequalities** and, as you have seen, they can be studied at any scale from global to local.

## Activities

1. Look at photograph **A** and discuss the inequalities that people living here might experience.

2. List the inequalities that can be seen in your own community. Find or take a photograph and annotate it to show these.

3. Using your ideas from questions **1** and **2**, brainstorm what might cause such inequalities. Draw a spider diagram to record your thoughts. Start your diagram with 'Causes of Inequality' in the centre box.

4. Good geographers should look for linkages between different causes, as well as for individual causes. Try to make some linkages in your spider diagram. For example, lack of education often makes it harder to find employment, so 'poor education' and 'unemployment' could be linked by an arrow.

5. Twenty-two per cent of the world's population live on less than US $1 (about 65p) per day. Think about what you could buy with this money. Make a poster to educate others in your school about poverty.

### help!

Not all of your ideas are necessarily linked. Others could have several links or be linked in both directions. Think carefully before you mark on the linkages.

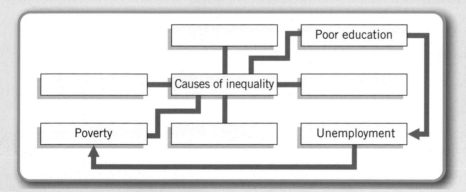

## Getting Technical

- **Gross National Product (GNP):** The value of the goods and services produced by a country and the income it earns from overseas. This is measured in US dollars (US $) and is often divided by the population to produce a measure called *GNP per capita*.

- **Human Development Index (HDI):** The HDI is used by the United Nations Development Programme (UNDP) to measure development. It is worked out by combining three different indicators: life expectancy, education levels, and income per person. The HDI has a value between 0 and 1 – a higher value means a higher level of human development.

# Mapping development

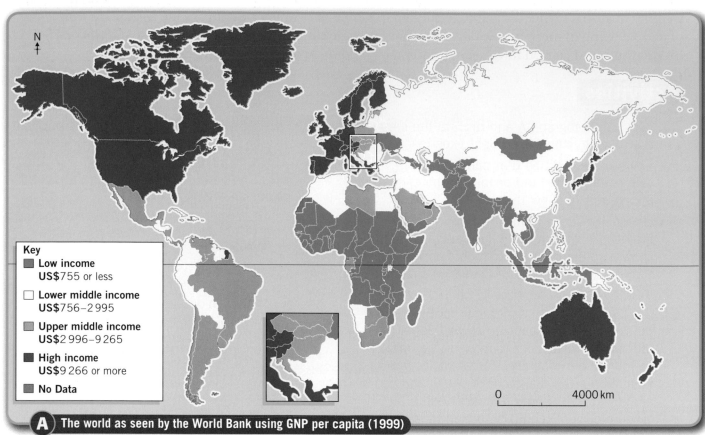

**Key**

- **Low income**
  US$755 or less
- **Lower middle income**
  US$756–2 995
- **Upper middle income**
  US$2 996–9 265
- **High income**
  US$9 266 or more
- **No Data**

0        4000 km

**A** The world as seen by the World Bank using GNP per capita (1999)

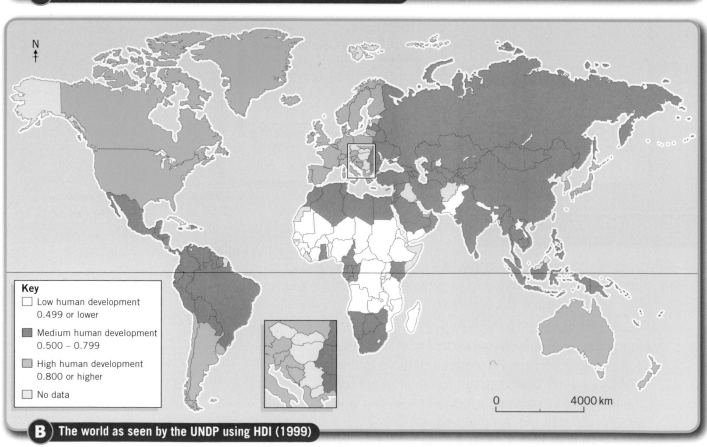

**Key**

- Low human development
  0.499 or lower
- Medium human development
  0.500 – 0.799
- High human development
  0.800 or higher
- No data

0        4000 km

**B** The world as seen by the UNDP using HDI (1999)

Different aspects of development in any one place can be measured using **development indicators**. Many different indicators can be used – so the pattern of development varies, depending on which indicator is chosen.

The World Bank measures development using Gross National Product (GNP) per capita. It uses this measure to divide the world into four different groups of countries: low income, lower-middle income, upper-middle income and high income. According to this method, Luxembourg was the most developed country and Ethiopia the least developed in 1999. Map **A** on page 12 shows how the World Bank views the world.

The United Nations Development Programme (UNDP) uses the Human Development Index (HDI) to measure development. Using the HDI, the UNDP divides the world into three groups of countries: low, medium and high human development. By this measure, Norway was the most developed country and Sierra Leone the least developed in 1999. Map **B** shows how the world looks when measured using the HDI.

## Activities

**1** Use a blank map of the world and an atlas.

**a** Find the countries mentioned on this page and mark them on your map.

**b** Choose a way to show the World Bank and UNDP methods of measuring development and use it for the countries you have marked.

**c** Choose four more countries from map **A** with low income, lower-middle income, upper-middle income and high income and add them to your map using your chosen method.

**d** Choose six more countries from map **B** with high, medium or low human development and add them to your map using your chosen method.

**2** Write a geographical description of world development using the same terms that are used by the World Bank and UNDP. Include countries or regions as examples. You may use the writing frame below to guide you.

> World Development can be looked at in different ways.
> The World Bank measures development …
>
> By contrast, the United Nations …
>
> Although the two measures are different, they are alike in some interesting ways.
> For example, some countries …
>
> Other countries …
>
> Another similarity I notice is …
>
> However, there are also some important differences.
>
> For example …
>
> To sum up, when we describe world development …

**3** Choose one more developed country and one less developed country. Find out as much as you can about your chosen country using the Internet or books.

**4** Design a poster comparing development in the two countries you have chosen. Make sure you include information about wealth, quality of life, and inequalities. Include any other information that you think is relevant.

**5** Add any new key words from pages 7 to 13 to your word bank.

### help!

The following websites can be linked to through www.heinemann.co.uk/hotlinks They contain information about the countries of the world and could be a useful starting point for your research.

○ United Nations Schools site

○ Social Watch country data

○ Central Intelligence Agency

○ Fact Monster Learning Network.

Remember to look for your own useful websites too.

# Inequalities in development

The statistics used to measure a country's level of development are averages, so they often hide large variations in the real situation of people living there. Table **A** shows the differences in income between the richest 20 per cent and the poorest 20 per cent of the population in five countries.

| Country | Poorest 20 per cent | Richest 20 per cent |
|---------|--------------------|--------------------|
| Brazil | $578 | $18563 |
| Kenya | $238 | $4347 |
| India | $527 | $2641 |
| UK | $3963 | $38164 |
| USA | $5800 | $51705 |

 **A** Incomes in US dollars (US $) per year

*Source: UNDP, 1999*

## Activities

**1 a** Make a copy of table **B**.

**b** Calculate how big the inequality is between the poorest and richest 20 per cent of the population. Write your answer as a ratio figure. The first one has been done for you (the 'How to' box will also help).

| Country | Poorest 20 per cent | Richest 20 per cent | Ratio of richest to poorest |
|---------|--------------------|--------------------|-----------------------------|
| Brazil | 578 | 18 563 | 32:1 |
|  |  |  |  |

**B**

**2 Extension**

Use a spreadsheet package to do the calculations in activity **1** and show your results as a graph. Think carefully about how best to present the information. (ICT)

**3** Describe what your results from activity **1** show you. For example, which is the most equal country and which has the greatest inequalities? Your work from page 11 might also help you to explain your findings.

**4** What have you learned about the value of using averages to measure development?

## How to ...

**... calculate ratios**

1 To calculate the ratio, divide the larger figure by the smaller figure.

2 The result tells you how many times greater the largest figure is than the smaller figure – the ratio.

3 For example with Brazil:
18563 ÷ 578 = 32.11 so the richest 20 per cent earn 32 times more than the poorest 20 per cent.

4 When writing the ratio, round your result to the nearest whole number, in this example: 32.

# Contrasting lifestyles in Kenya

## Case Study: Alice

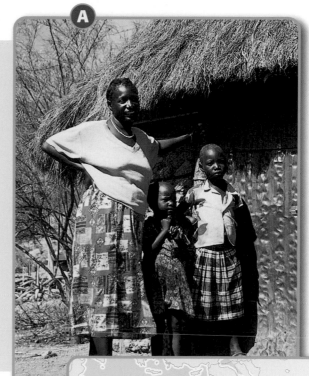

My name is Alice and I live here in the West Pokot region of Western Kenya with my husband and four children. I have had seven children in total, but three died before they were even five years old – I was very sad. In our community nearly 150 out of every 1000 children born will die before their fifth birthday. I hope to enrol my children in primary school this year, but it is expensive. My brother has ten children, but only three of them go to primary school. We just don't have enough money – we have just a few goats and our land is not good for farming. Last year we earned just US $120 as a family, even with my husband working at a nearby agricultural project.

## Case Study: Christopher

I'm Christopher and I work for a travel company in Nairobi. We take tourists to see our wonderful wildlife and spectacular scenery. It is a good job and last year I earned US $2 640, which is much more than I could earn back in my village. It is still difficult to support my wife and two children, however, especially as she is not working at the moment. She insists on looking after our younger child. So many children die when they are young, but the clinic we go to is very modern and loses only 24 per 1000 before they are five, so we are hopeful. If I keep my job, I will be able to send both my children to primary school, but if we have any more children it could be difficult to educate them all.

C Kenya

## Activities

**1** Carefully read the case studies of Alice and Christopher. They represent differences in the quality of life in Kenya.

**2** Using data from both case studies calculate the average level of:

**a** income per person (GNP per capita)

**b** under-five mortality rate (U5MR)

**c** primary school enrolment.

**3** The data has been adjusted so that the values you calculate represent the national average for Kenya in 1997. In reality you would need a full data set to calculate averages like these. Copy out a table like the one below with seven rows. You could use a spreadsheet for this task. Enter your data for Kenya in the first row. (ICT)

### How to ...

**... calculate averages**

To calculate the average of several values:

**1** Work out the values for each example (in this case, Alice and Christopher).

**2** Add these values together.

**3** Divide the total by the number of values (in this case two values – one for each case study).

For example, to work out the average GNP per capita:

US $20 (Alice) + US $660 (Christopher) = US $680

US $680 ÷ 2 = US $340

Remember, their salaries have to be divided by the number of people in the family.

| Country | Average income (GNP per capita) | Under-five mortality rate (per 1000 born) | Primary school enrolment (%) |
|---------|--------------------------------|-------------------------------------------|------------------------------|
| Kenya | | | |
| | | | |

**4** Add the other countries from page 14 into your table and use the Social Watch website (through www.heinemann.co.uk/hotlinks) to find the data for those countries. Use the menus on screen to select your data, countries and year. (ICT)

**5** If you have not already done so, find the same information for the countries you selected in question **3** on page 13. Add this to your table.

**6** Put all seven countries into rank order for each of the development indicators. If you have used a spreadsheet, use the computer to do this. Does the order of countries vary much? (ICT)

**7** **Extension**

Using the Social Watch on-line database, make up your own data tables to compare different development issues for the countries in your table. You could also expand your research to include other countries – for example, one from each continent. (ICT)

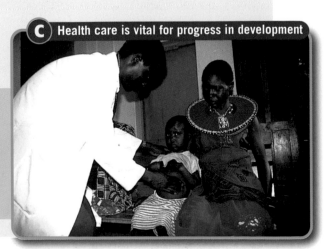
**C** Health care is vital for progress in development

# Progress in development

In the second half of the twentieth century significant progress was made in world development. For example, life expectancy increased from a global average of 45 years in 1950 to about 67 years at the start of the year 2000. Improvements in health care and higher levels of education have been two of the main developments responsible for this progress. But just as development levels vary between countries and regions, so too does progress in development. Some regions have improved rapidly while other regions show little progress at all. Table **B** shows the progress in development for the world's major regions between 1970 and 1998.

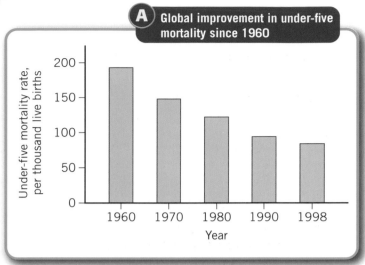

**A** Global improvement in under-five mortality since 1960

*Source: United Nations*

| Region | Life expectancy (years) | | Adult literacy rate (%) | | Under-five mortality rate | |
| --- | --- | --- | --- | --- | --- | --- |
| | 1970 | 1998 | 1970 | 1998 | 1970 | 1998 |
| Sub-Saharan Africa | 45 | 49 | 29 | 58.5 | 226 | 172 |
| Arab States | 52 | 66 | 31.3 | 59.7 | 193 | 72 |
| East Asia | 63 | 70 | 81.5 | 83.4 | 118 | 46 |
| South-East Asia | 55 | 66 | 56.3 | 88.2 | 149 | 57 |
| South Asia | 50 | 63 | 33.8 | 54.3 | 206 | 106 |
| Latin America and the Caribbean | 61 | 69 | 72.5 | 87.7 | 123 | 39 |
| Eastern Europe and former USSR | 69 | 69 | 96.1 | 98.6 | 47 | 33 |
| Industrialised countries | 70 | 76 | 97 | 97.4 | 52 | 14 |
| World | 60 | 67 | n/a | 78.8 | 148 | 84 |

**B** Progress in development between 1970 and 1998

*Data taken from UNICEF 1996 and UNDP 2000*

## Activities

❶ Using the data in table **B**, calculate the percentage change in each indicator for the world's major regions. This is a long job, so work in a group or use a spreadsheet package to help you. (1)(2)(3)

❷ Look at your results for activity **1**.

  **a** Which regions have seen the greatest progress and which the least?

  **b** Which indicator has shown most progress and which the least?

❸ Using a blank map of the world, work out a way to show your results from **1** and **2**. Think carefully about the best way to show change.

❹ Imagine you are advising on where development efforts should be focused in the future. Using your results from **1** and **2**, write a proposal suggesting what the focus should be and which regions should be targeted as a priority.

## Case Study

### Who decides?

| | Percentage involved on regular basis |
|---|---|
| Men | 6 |
| Boys (15–18 years) | 11 |
| Boys (under 15 years) | 34 |
| Women | 94 |
| Girls (15–18 years) | 83 |
| Girls (under 15 years) | 62 |

**C** Water collection as part of daily activities in Kenya

**A** Collecting water in Kenya

**B** Location of proposed borehole in Maruni village

Proposed well site · Shops · School · Clinic · Road · River · Water table level · N

# Water boost for West Pokot village

Maruni villagers received welcome news today when plans to develop a borehole in their village were announced. Pokot elders finalised plans yesterday with Joseph Lomaria from the regional development authority, who will provide technical assistance, and Philip Saunders, from a UK charity that is funding the project.

Village meetings to discuss water supply problems identified the need for a borehole. At present water is collected from the nearby river, but this is hard work and wastes valuable time. Clean water is found in the rocks under the entire village, but elders decided to drill the borehole in the eastern side of the village where they felt it was most needed.

The local health worker welcomed the announcement. She hopes that a safe water supply would reduce water-related diseases, but stresses the important part played by education in reducing these diseases. She seemed surprised that she had not been consulted on the plans.

The new borehole will be drilled next month and should be in use by the end of the year. There are plans to develop more boreholes if tensions between the Pokot and neighbouring Turkana people subside.

**D** News extract, 9 October 2000

Collecting water is hard work, but I don't mind it because I get to meet and talk with my friends. We can talk about school. If it took less time to collect water I would just be given another job to do.
**(Alice, aged 15)**

I remember before people lived here when we used to visit with our cattle. When the river was low we would dig holes to get to the water for our cattle, but up here the water holes would dry up in the dry season and we would have to get water from over there, the other side of the village.
**(Mzee, old Turkana man from east of village)**

I attended the village meetings, but women are not free to speak, we would be told to just keep quiet and let the men make the decisions.
**(Perpetua, 34 years old)**

I hear what they have said, but do not always agree. When you are young, though, you cannot argue even if you have a better idea.
**(Joshua, aged 13)**

**E** The views of some local people

## Activities

**1 a** Make a list of the key groups involved in the development project in Maruni village. Be careful to include all those involved in the project and all those who might be affected by it.

**b** Make a card for each group involved and label it with their group name, for example *Women, Elders*.

**c** Copy a ladder onto a blank piece of paper. Draw one rung (step) of the ladder for each of the cards you have made.

**d** Taking each card in turn, arrange them in order of the group's participation and decision-making in the project. Put those who are least involved at the bottom of the ladder and those who are most involved at the top of the ladder.

**e** Write the groups onto your ladder.

**2** Take the cards away and repeat the exercise. This time, put the groups in the order that you think they *should* be in. Remember to justify your order.

**3** Compare your new ladder with the first one you recorded. What are the key differences?

**4** Repeat the activity for a local development issue in your own community, perhaps one that includes you. Remember to include all those who are involved.

### help!

- Keep moving your cards until you are happy that you have the groups in the order you want.

- You may think that some groups need to share a rung on the ladder.

# Sustainable development

**A** Clear-cut forestry (where all the trees are cut down) in British Columbia, Canada

**B** Reforestation in the Sudan, Africa

Development does not always bring benefits, especially for the environment. Short-term benefits for some people – jobs and income – often turn into longer-term costs for many people and the environment. For example, the development of the logging and timber industry has led to large-scale deforestation and environmental degradation.

Policies for sustainable development have been introduced by many governments and companies. For example, the Forestry Stewardship Council (see **C**) monitors the number of trees being cut down and ensures that an equal number are planted to provide timber for future generations.

Not all development is sustainable, however. Many development projects continue to threaten the environment today and for future generations. For example, using fossil fuels for energy causes problems such as acid rain and releases large quantities of carbon dioxide ($CO_2$) – a greenhouse gas responsible for global warming. Fossil fuels are also formed over millions of years, meaning that they cannot be replaced for future generations.

**FSC** ©

**C**

**Sustainable Development** is development that meets the needs of the present without compromising the ability of future generations to meet their own needs.

**D** From *Our Common Future* World Commission on Environment and Development, 1987

**E** There are many different types of development

## Activities

1. Study the drawings in **E**. Working in a pair or small group, decide which developments you think are sustainable and which are not. Give reasons for your decisions, using evidence to support your argument.

2. Look again at the other examples of development in this unit, including those you have found for your local area. Repeat activity **1** for those.

3. Imagine you are responsible for improving sustainable development. Looking at those projects you have listed as unsustainable, what alternatives might you recommend?

4. Create and carry out a research project to investigate how sustainable your school is.

   **a** List the sustainable and unsustainable examples that you find.

   **b** Make a series of recommendations to improve sustainability in your school. Include reasons for your proposed actions and suggest who is responsible for implementing them.

5. Using what you have learned about sustainable development, design a poster to promote the benefits of sustainable development and the actions that individuals can take.

6. **Extension**

   Imagine that you can travel forward in time. Write a description of life in the year 2050 if development follows a sustainable path. Then write a description of how life might be if sustainable development is ignored. You could write your description as a short story, a newspaper article, or a poem.

# Review and reflect

## Development into the twenty-first century

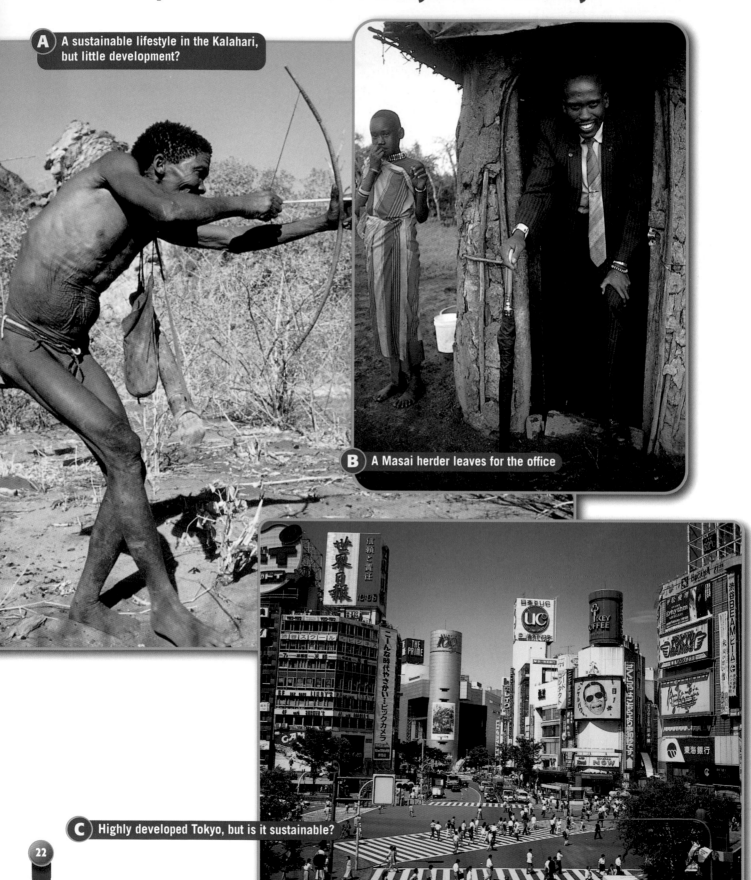

**A** A sustainable lifestyle in the Kalahari, but little development?

**B** A Masai herder leaves for the office

**C** Highly developed Tokyo, but is it sustainable?

As you have learned in this unit, life for most of the world's population improved significantly during the twentieth century. On the whole, people lived longer and were healthier than ever before. However, you have also seen that progress has not been equal and that many people and places still suffer poverty and low standards of living. There are also new concerns about the ability of our planet to support continued progress. People are calling for a rethink about development to make it more sustainable. International targets have been set and development partners, from global institutions to local communities, are working to try to meet those targets. But there is still much to be done. The pace of change remains slow, and it is doubtful that many of the targets will be met on time. So development needs to be a priority for everyone if sustainability is to become a reality in the early part of the twenty-first century.

## Activities

1. Look back at the photos in this unit. Working in a pair or small group, select an image that represents one of the key challenges and priorities for development into the twenty-first century.

2. Use the report framework below to plan and write a development report about your chosen image. Include relevant data, words and terms from the unit or from your own research. Remember that you can add your own questions to the framework.

   - What is your chosen development challenge/priority?
   - Why is it a challenge/priority?
   - Where is this challenge/priority most important?
   - What actions need to be taken to meet your challenge/priority?
   - Who should take responsibility and why?
   - What should their target be (what is to be done and by when)?
   - What might get in the way and how might this be resolved?
   - How realistic is it that your challenge/priority will be met on target?
   - Why did you choose that particular issue?

3. Working with your partner or group, prepare a short presentation for the class to explain the key findings of your report. Remember to be prepared to answer any questions they might have.

4. Finally, complete your word bank for this unit with new words and terms from pages 14 to 23.

# 2 France

## The changing economic geography of France

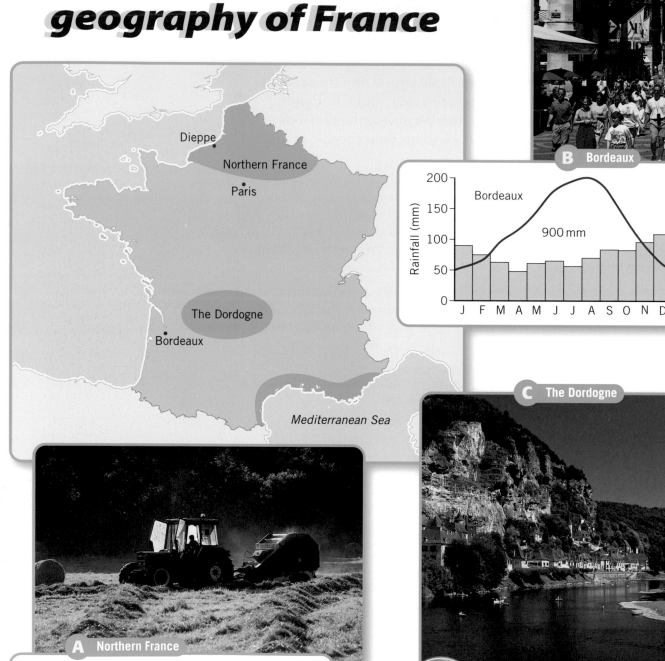

Dieppe

Northern France

Paris

The Dordogne

Bordeaux

Mediterranean Sea

**B** Bordeaux

Bordeaux

900 mm

Rainfall (mm)

Temperature (°C)

J F M A M J J A S O N D

**C** The Dordogne

**A** Northern France

Northern France

727 mm

Rainfall (mm)

Temperature (°C)

J F M A M J J A S O N D

## Learn about

In this unit you will focus on France and learn about:

⊚ patterns of economic activity in France

⊚ how economic activities are changing

⊚ the impact of changing economic activities

⊚ the economic links with other countries.

E  Dieppe

Mediterranean

546 mm

D  The Mediterranean

F  Paris

Paris

619 mm

## Activities

1. **a** Study the photographs and climate graphs of France.

   **b** Copy and complete the table below to describe the physical and human features of France.

   **c** Research, using an atlas, the weather for **C** and **F**.

| | Photo A | Photo B | Photo C |
|---|---|---|---|
| Physical/natural features (e.g. mountains, rivers, trees, hills) Climate (e.g. hot, rainy, sunny) | | | |
| Economic activity (e.g. farming, industry, services) | | | |
| Settlement (e.g. flats, houses, village, city) | | | |
| Population (e.g. lots of people, few people, farmers, tourists) | | | |

2. Use the information in your table. Is there a link between the economic activities of France and the physical environment?

### Getting Technical

- **Economic activities** are work or activities that people earn money from.

- **Primary activities** are activities that extract natural resources from the earth or sea.

- **Secondary activities** are activities that process raw materials from primary activities to produce finished goods or semi-finished goods.

- **Tertiary activities** are activities that provide a service.

# What is France's economy like? How is it changing?

**A** Harvesting

**B** Aeronautics industry

**C** Café in Paris

Large-scale ship building

Families run farms

Electronics

People are leaving the land

Mining is beginning to decline

Higher employment in primary sector

Recruitment firms expand

Wealth is increasing

Labour-intensive farming

Using computers

**1970s**

**2000**

Fewer services

Many fishermen employed

Small shops

High-tech research

Growth in services continues

Robotics and robots rule

Increased economic wealth

Working in hotels/tourism

**D** Changing economic activities in France

## Activities

**1** Match the economic activities in photos **A**, **B** and **C** into primary, secondary and tertiary activities.

**2** Classify the phrases in **D** into those that relate to the 1970s and those that relate to 2000.

**3** Using your classification, describe how economic activities in the 1970s were different from those in 2000.

**E** Average annual income

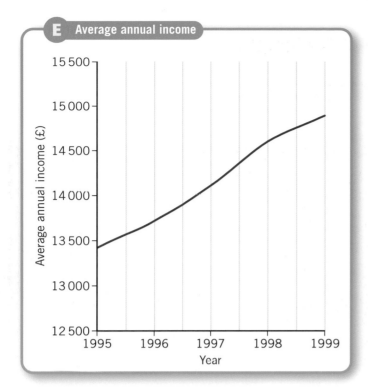

| | Oil | Gas | Coal | Electricity | Others |
|---|---|---|---|---|---|
| Production | 99 | 35 | 14 | 92 | 11 |
| Consumption | 93 | 34 | 7 | 32 | 9 |

*Figures in million tonnes of oil equivalent*
*(ask your teacher if you do not understand this).*

**F** Energy production and consumption in France, 1999

The number of people out of work in France is high – over 11 per cent of the total working population. The situation is even worse than it appears because:

⊚ many young people stay in education for a long time

⊚ many people are doing their military service.

One reason for unemployment in France is that there are not enough people with the right skills for the jobs available. However, between now and 2010 the number of unemployed people in France will probably fall.

| | 1995 | 1996 | 1997 | 1998 | 1999 |
|---|---|---|---|---|---|
| Number registered unemployed (thousands) | 3000 | 3100 | 3100 | 3000 | 2800 |
| Unemployment rate (%) | 11.6 | 12.3 | 12.5 | 11.8 | 11.2 |

**G** Unemployment statistics

## Activities ①②③

① Study graph **E**.
   **a** What was the average income in 1999?
   **b** What has been the increase in average income between 1995 and 1999?
   **c** Between which two years was the biggest increase in annual income?
   **d** Write a sentence to explain the patterns that the graph shows.

② Use the data in table **F** to draw a bar chart showing the production and consumption of each type of energy. Copy the outline below and use different colours to show production and consumption, label the axes and add a title at the top of the chart.

③ Read the paragraph above on the right. Use this and the unemployment statistics in table **G** to create a five-minute news flash about unemployment in France.

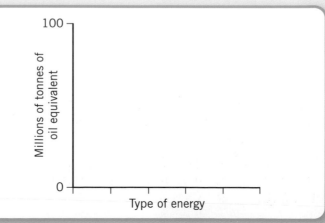

# What changes have occurred in the agricultural industry?

## Agriculture in France

France has the biggest agricultural industry in Europe. It is the second biggest exporter of agricultural produce in the world behind the USA.

For the past fifty years the number of farmers has been decreasing. In 1970 there were 2.8 million farmers and in 1998 there were just 1.1 million. During the 1990s, 30 000 farmers gave up farming each year.

Despite there being fewer farmers, production has increased. In the 1940s one farmer could produce enough food to feed five people but by 1990 one farmer could produce enough food to feed 30 people.

Production has increased for a number of reasons, including more intensive farming techniques and the use of fertilisers and pesticides.

**A** An upland farm

France's farming industry has benefited from the support of the European Union. Farmers are given a guaranteed price for their produce as well as grants to help them in many other ways.

However, guaranteed prices meant that farmers were paid money to produce more food, and too much food was produced. This resulted in the 'milk lakes' and 'butter mountains' of the 1980s.

Because of this over-production, support from the European Union is now being reduced. This is resulting in problems in France because the support favours the most efficient farmers who are often the richest and need the least help.

**B** Intensive farming

## Activities

1 Read the information about farming in France. Choose five phrases from the text above about changes in agriculture and use them to complete the sentence below:

Agriculture in France is changing ...

2 **a** In groups of four, consider the following question. You may use the information on this page and the statements on the opposite page, or any knowledge you have about agriculture in France.

Why is the number of farmers in France going down but production is increasing?

**b** Make a short summary or presentation of your ideas.

Pierre has been adding fertilisers to his crops since 1980.

Jean Claude is guaranteed a set price for all his cows.

Irrigation means that more crops can be grown.

Machinery has made farming a lot quicker.

**In 1950 there were 2.3 million farms. In 1990 there were 900 000.**

Fabien, my son, lost his job because the farm he worked on bought new machinery.

Guaranteed prices from the European Union have led to over-production.

We use only natural fertilisers on our crops.

There is increasing demand for organically grown food.

Because I use pesticides I lose less of my produce as the bugs that eat the crops are killed.

Seeds and plants are more resistant to diseases now because of genetic engineering.

In 1950 the average farm size was 14 hectares. In 1990 it was 36 hectares.

Advances in technology mean that fewer farmers are needed.

In 1950 there were 5.1 million people working in farming compared to 1.1 million in 1998.

Wine makes up a lot of farming exports for France.

**The fishing industry is suffering because of cheap imports.**

Fewer farmers are needed now because machines are quicker.

Many people have left their farms to work in the city.

Woodland covers a quarter of France. Some timber is exported but even more is imported.

We are the only family-run farm for 10 km.

Selective breeding programmes mean that only the best animals are produced on my farm.

# What changes have occurred in manufacturing industry?

## Case Study

**A** Grenoble is located in the Rhône-Alpes region

Rhône-Alpes
Grenoble

## Getting Technical ▼

A **technopole** is an area with new high-tech industries.

## Activities

**1** Study the broken sentences in boxes **B** and **C**. To find out *how* and *why* manufacturing industry in the Rhône-Alpes region of France has changed, match the starts of the sentences in box **B** with the endings in box **C**.

**2** Imagine you have been sent to interview M. Charvet, the owner of a micro-electronics manufacturing company in Grenoble. You have completed the interview (see box **D**) but have forgotten to write down the questions you asked. Write the questions to match the answers from the interview. The first one has been completed for you.

**3** **Extension**
Imagine you are a reporter for a British newspaper and your editor has sent you to France to report on industry in the Rhône-Alpes region.

**a** Use a desktop publishing or word-processing package to complete this activity.
**b** The headline is 'Out with the old, in with the new!'
**c** Lay out your work to look like a real newspaper article. Make up a suitable name for your newspaper and include the headline and your name on the page.
**d** Use the following paragraph plan when writing your article:

◎ First paragraph: Say why, what, where, when and who.
◎ Second paragraph: Give more details about the five points above, and say how.
◎ Third paragraph: Use a quote from your interview with M. Charvet in Activity 2.
◎ Fourth, fifth and sixth paragraphs: Include other details from Activity 1.
◎ Seventh and eighth paragraphs: Write a suitable conclusion.

**B**

*Old heavy industries have been in decline in the region since the oil*

**Technopoles were set up in Rhône-Alpes**

**People who did work in the old industries rarely work in the**

**Technopoles make good profits so**

The government has helped the region by giving

*Transport routes are good and provide a link between northern and*

The Rhône-Alpes region is France's leading producer of

*New high-tech industries locate in areas called*

**C**

technopoles, which are like science parks.

money to improve housing and roads.

region in the 1980s.

southern Europe.

they can pay more for rent and taxes.

new industries because they do not have the skills.

manufactured goods.

*crisis of 1979.*

**D**

You: *Where and when did you start up your company?*

M. Charvet: I built my micro-electronics factory on the technopole in Grenoble, which is in the Rhône-Alpes region, back in 1986.

You:

M. Charvet: I previously owned a factory which produced oil-based products.

You:

M. Charvet: I was affected by a range of issues – my company didn't recover from the oil crisis of 1979.

You:

M. Charvet: The technopole is a great area to locate – it benefits from being at the centre of networks of motorways, high-speed railways and air routes.

You:

M. Charvet: You can also find the Nuclear Research Centre, the World Health Organization and the Cancer Research Centre here.

You:

M. Charvet: The Lorraine and Nord regions have also suffered from a decline in traditional manufacturing industries.

You:

M. Charvet: The future is bright because the government is actually encouraging technopoles to develop.

# What is the pattern of tourism in France?

## Activities

### A trip to France

- At last! The holidays are here and you are off to travel around France for a fortnight.

- You have been planning your route for months and have investigated six tourist areas in France.

- You will fly from Birmingham to Paris, and catch the ferry home from Calais.

**1** You need to choose five areas to visit from the choice of six. You must visit Paris and Boulogne.

**2** You need to pack for the trip. Your bag must not weigh more than 6.5 kg (6 500 g) when it is full.

**3** For each stage of your journey you need to:
  a Decide what you will pack and why. Use table **A** to help you.
  b Decide what you want to see and do at each location and why.
  c Calculate the distances between your destinations using table **B**.
  d Decide how long you will stay at each location and why.

## Boulogne

Average July temperature: 22 °C
- White cliffs similar to those at Dover run along the coast between Boulogne and Calais.
- Boulogne's historic buildings include the Palais de Justice, the library and the town hall.
- The wide range of restaurants and shops are well worth a visit.
- Will you visit local hypermarkets before you catch the ferry?

## La Rochelle

Average July temperature: 25 °C
- La Rochelle is well known for its historic port.
- The marina is the busiest yachting centre on the French Atlantic.
- Countless cafés and restaurants cluster around the waterfront.
- The cobbled streets of the old town are lined with boutiques.
- The fifteenth-century prison is worth a visit. It has amazing views from the tower.
- You could visit the modern aquarium.

Birmingham

Calais

Boulogne

**Key**
— High-speed lines
— Standard lines

N

Paris

La Rochelle

The Alps

0    100 km

Toulouse

Nice

## Toulouse

Average July temperature: 25 °C
- The birthplace of Concorde.
- An important industrial and university city.
- You may want to visit Pont Neuf on the River Garonne.
- Tourists are drawn to the two thirteenth-century cathedrals.
- The old town has a lively atmosphere and inexpensive cafés.
- A flea market is held every Sunday.

# Paris

Average July temperature: 24 °C

- The spectacular city of Paris has something to offer everyone: from chic shopping to spectacular shows, Paris has it all.
- Paris is the capital of France and the home of fashion.
- The city's highlights include a stroll along the Champs-Élysées from the Arc de Triomphe towards the Louvre, where you could see the *Mona Lisa*.
- You might want to visit the Eiffel Tower or the modern art gallery called Musée d'Orsay.
- You could eat in a gourmet restaurant or enjoy a dinner cruise on the River Seine.

# The Alps

Average July temperature: 28 °C

- Stunning scenery combined with fine hospitality.
- From foothills to dramatic peaks, the Alps are a magnet for visitors in summer and winter.
- Skiers need no introduction to this winter playground.
- You might want to try mountain biking or horse riding in the hills.

# Nice

Average July temperature: 28 °C

- The two-kilometre golden beach of Nice has to be seen.
- The promenade is lined with palms and has wonderful views.
- The old town has a blend of balconied buildings, and is home to artists, galleries, boutiques and, of course, restaurants.
- You could visit the market.
- You could relax in a pavement café and spend your time people-watching!

| Item | Weight (g) | Item | Weight (g) |
|------|-----------|------|-----------|
| Water bottle | 50 | Raincoat | 300 |
| Money belt | 50 | Washing kit | 300 |
| Sunglasses | 50 | Sleeping bag | 350 |
| Socks | 50 | Long skirt | 350 |
| Swimsuit/trunks | 100 | Towel | 400 |
| Pack of cards | 150 | Tracksuit bottoms | 400 |
| Deodorant | 150 | Suntan lotion | 400 |
| Hair gel/spray | 200 | Shampoo | 400 |
| Aftershave/perfume | 200 | Dress | 450 |
| Underwear | 200 | Smart trousers | 450 |
| Umbrella | 200 | Camera and film | 500 |
| Shirt/blouse | 200 | Hairdryer | 500 |
| Mountain kit | 200 | Sleeping mat | 500 |
| Sarong | 200 | Fleece | 600 |
| Sandals | 200 | Jeans | 600 |
| Shorts | 250 | Smart shoes | 700 |
| T-shirt | 250 | Jumper | 700 |
| Thermals | 250 | Trainers | 800 |
| Make-up bag | 250 | Travel guide | 1000 |
| Book | 300 | Walking boots | 1000 |

**A** Travel kit weight guide

| | Boulogne | La Rochelle | Toulouse | Paris | Alps | Nice |
|---|---|---|---|---|---|---|
| **Boulogne** | | 350 | 700 | 250 | 550 | 800 |
| **La Rochelle** | 350 | | 325 | 350 | 550 | 625 |
| **Toulouse** | 700 | 325 | | 475 | 400 | 375 |
| **Paris** | 250 | 350 | 475 | | 350 | 550 |
| **Alps** | 550 | 550 | 400 | 350 | | 300 |
| **Nice** | 800 | 625 | 375 | 550 | 300 | |

**B** Chart to show distances between possible destinations (km)

## Activity

**4** **Extension**

After your trip you could evaluate your holiday to make next year's journey even better. Use the following sentence starters to help you.

I enjoyed …

As well …

I have learnt that …

Skills I have used include …

For example …

I had a problem with …

Next year I would …

## Case Study

# Tourism in Rhône-Alpes

It is estimated that 60 million tourists visit France every year, and some of these will visit the Rhône-Alpes region. The Rhône-Alpes region is partly made up of the Alps, but these are just one of the region's tourist attractions. The region attracts tourists in both summer and winter for a number of reasons.

In the east of the region are the Alps and tourists come to ski and snowboard in the winter and walk in the summer.

Tourists come all year round to visit the River Rhône, where they can enjoy lots of watersports and river walks. The area is also famous for its vineyards.

In the south of the region is the Ardèche Gorge, home to many prehistoric caves. The famous Combe d'Arc cave has drawings that are 20 000 years old.

People also come to the region to visit the major cities. In the cities of Grenoble and Lyons tourists soak up the culture by visiting the museums and art galleries as well as eating in the many restaurants and cafés.

**A** The River Rhône

## Activities

**1** Read the information about tourism in the Rhône-Alpes region.

**a** In one colour, identify five things to do and see in Rhône-Alpes.

**b** In another colour, identify five facts about tourism in Rhône-Alpes.

**2** In groups of three, take the role of one of the following characters each and present/discuss his or her views about tourism in Rhône-Alpes:

- ⊚ tourist (skier)
- ⊚ environmentalist
- ⊚ business person (for example, hotel or shop owner)
- ⊚ local resident
- ⊚ local councillor.

The three characters should have a conversation about tourism in Rhône-Alpes. Your conversation should be based around the following points:

- ⊚ whether your character thinks tourism is a good idea
- ⊚ what your character thinks about the effects that tourism has on the environment
- ⊚ your character's opinion about the money tourism brings in to the area.

# What energy resources does France have?

France as a nation uses many different types of energy. This energy comes from a range of sources.

From Algeria

From Middle East

Dunkirk

From Netherlands and North Sea

Nord

From Former USSR

Petit-Couronne

From Africa    Le Havre

Lorraine

St-Laurent

Dampierre

From Algeria

Denges

Blanzy

Bugey

Feyzin

Carmaux

Lacq

Marseilles

From Algeria    From Middle East and Africa

**Key**
- ➤ Natural gas imports
- ■ Natural gas source (in France)
- ● Natural gas port
- ➤ Oil imports
- ■ Oil refinery
- ■ Nuclear power station
- ■ Hydroelectric power station
- ● Coalfield
- ■ Coal-fired power station

**A** The location of France's energy sources

## Coal

- ◉ Coal was a very important source of energy in France until recently.

- ◉ In 1958, 60 million tonnes were produced – 60 per cent of the total energy used in France.

- ◉ In 1958, 300 000 miners were employed.

- ◉ By 1989, only 13 million tonnes were produced each year and only 28 000 miners were employed.

- ◉ The last mine on one of the main coalfields, Nord-Pas-de-Calais, closed in 1991. It was expensive to mine coal there and the type of coal was bad for the miners' health. The environment in this area has been badly affected by spoil tips, derelict mine buildings, and water and air pollution.

**B** Coal mining in France

35

# Hydroelectric power (HEP)

- HEP has been welcomed by many people in France as it is a non-polluting source of energy.

- HEP has been developed in the mountains of France where many of the fast-flowing rivers are dammed.

- HEP is a renewable type of energy, so it will never run out.

- The use of water power to produce energy has been slow to develop for a number of reasons:

  - Only small amounts of energy can be produced from each HEP plant.

  - Some people think the plants spoil the landscape where they are constructed.

  - In the years 1989 to 1990 HEP was badly affected by a drought which greatly reduced output.

**C** Dam at Tignes, France

# Gas and oil

- Gas and oil are important sources of energy and both are used to generate electricity.

- Gas and oil are both fossil fuels and have two main disadvantages:

  - They are non-renewable (they will run out over time).

  - They cause air pollution.

- Most of the gas and oil used in France is imported from Russia and the Netherlands.

- Since the oil crises in the 1970s, France has cut back on its use of oil.

**D** Gas pipeline, Manosque

**E** Drilling for oil

# Nuclear power

◎ Nuclear power is the main source of France's energy resources.

◎ In 1974 the French government began to invest in nuclear power stations.

◎ It takes seven years to build a nuclear reactor, so it was not until the early 1980s that nuclear power could be used.

◎ There are problems regarding nuclear waste – where should it be stored?

◎ Nuclear power stations tend to be located near a water source, which is used for cooling.

**F** Nuclear power station at St Alban–St Maurice, on the River Rhône

◎ Nuclear power has its advantages – it is very efficient and relatively cheap to make.

◎ The cost of building nuclear power generators is huge. These costs have led to huge debts for Electricité de France. The state electricity company had a debt of £25.4 billion by 1990.

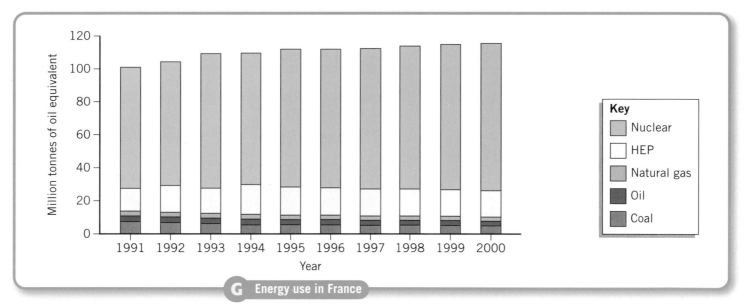

**G** Energy use in France

## Activities

❶ Using the information on each type of energy, create a timeline from 1958 to 2001 to show the changes in energy use in France.

❷ Copy and complete the table below to show the advantages and disadvantages of each type of energy.

| Energy source | Advantages | Disadvantages |
| --- | --- | --- |
|  |  |  |

❸ Using graph **G**, draw your own graph to estimate France's energy use between 2000 and 2010. Explain the energy use you have predicted.

# France's energy mix – the nuclear power debate

**B**

Nuclear power is now the main source of …

*A tidal power station has also been built …*

In 1974 the French government began to …

There are lots of problems connected with the storage of nuclear waste because …

Nuclear power stations tend to be located near a water …

*Nuclear power uses uranium – the amount needed is small …*

*HEP has been developed in the mountains …*

**Recently some people have started to worry about …**

**A** Nuclear power station in the Loire valley

**C**

**invest in nuclear power stations.**

*at Rance in Normandy.*

**energy in France today.**

whether nuclear power is safe.

*no one wants it in their neighbourhood.*

and the cost is relatively low.

*where many of the fast-flowing rivers are dammed.*

source, which is used for cooling.

## Activities

**1** Study the broken sentences in boxes **B** and **C**.

**a** Match the starts of the sentences in box **B** with the endings in box **C**.

**b** There are two sentences which have nothing to do with nuclear power. Find these 'odd ones out' and write them down in a separate list from the sentences about nuclear power.

**2** Read the newspaper article in box **D**. People have a wide range of views about any debate. Some views are based on fact, others on opinion, and some may be a mixture of both.

**a** Write down the facts in one colour and the opinions in another colour.

**b** Share your facts and opinions with others in your group. How did you decide what was a fact and what was an opinion?

# LIFE IN THE SHADOW OF A NUCLEAR POWER STATION

Back in 1952 Madame Goma bought a house in the town of Dampierre. Today, she has a very different neighbour …

I met Madame Goma at her home and we discussed how the energy situation in France had changed over time and how it had affected her life.

During the 1970s the French economy was negatively affected by two oil crises. In 1974 the French government decided to build 34 nuclear reactors, followed in 1976 by a further 20. Today nuclear energy represents 75 per cent of the country's electricity production.

I asked Madame Goma what it was like living next to a nuclear power station.

'I feel safe living next to the station because of the very high standard of nuclear safety at the site, and other similar sites in France. I often see officials from the Ministry of Health around the site checking for radioactive releases from the site.'

Madame Goma felt that the site had also had a negative impact upon her life. 'The value of my house has suffered because it is so close to the site, and the continual noise of vehicles in and out of the station is a nuisance.'

Nuclear power has been very successful in France and it seems that it is likely to be so in the future. However, this source of energy is always a controversial issue, having as many disadvantages as advantages.

I doubt that everyone shares the opinions of Madame Goma. I'm sure the nuclear debate will continue for many years to come.

**D**

## Activity

**3 Extension**

Using all of the information from these pages, write a newspaper article examining how people feel about the use of nuclear power in France. Write your article from the viewpoint of one of the following people:

- environmental campaigner
- government official
- official from the nuclear power plant
- a worker from one of the plants.

Remember that all these people are affected by nuclear power in different ways and they may have differing opinions on this source of energy.

**help!**

Use four sections to structure your article:

- *Introduction* – write a paragraph to explain what the newspaper report is about.
- *Background* – describe where, when and why nuclear power stations have been built.
- *Current situation* – describe in detail the current situation.
- *Closing statement* – what are the consequences and how are you affected by what has happened?

# International trade

International trade is the buying and selling of goods between countries. Goods brought into a country are called imports and goods sold to other countries are called exports. The difference between the value of imports and the value of exports is called the balance of trade. This may vary from year to year.

| Imports | Exports |
|---------|---------|
| 1 785 000 million francs | 1 834 000 million francs |

**A** The value or France's imports and exports in 1999

## Activities

1. Create a word bank of the key words and terms in the text above – *international trade, imports, exports* and *balance of trade.*

2. Work out France's balance of trade in 1999 by subtracting the value of imports from the value of exports.

3. In 1999 France had a positive balance of trade. Read the first paragraph again, then explain why the balance of trade shows France has a healthy economy.

## France's exports

The goods exported from France in 1999 are shown in graph **B**.

| | | % |
|---|---|---|
| Raw materials, metals, chemicals | | 32 |
| Machines and equipment for industry | | 25 |
| Consumer goods | | 14 |
| Cars and trucks | | 14 |
| Food industry products | | 9 |
| Farm, forestry and fishing products | | 4 |
| Energy products | | 2 |

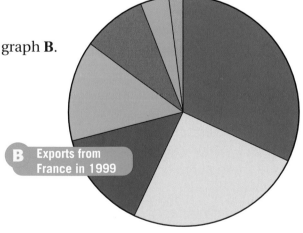

**B** Exports from France in 1999

France is famous for its exports of food products, clothes and cars. For example, nearly a quarter of cars sold in Europe are French. France's exports of high-tech goods are growing – an example is the aircraft industry, based at Toulouse.

# France's imports

| | | % |
|---|---|---|
| Raw materials, metals, chemicals | 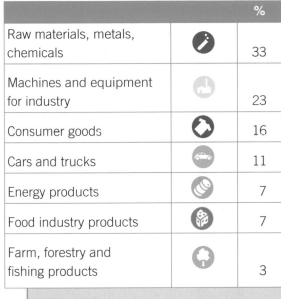 | 33 |
| Machines and equipment for industry | | 23 |
| Consumer goods | | 16 |
| Cars and trucks | | 11 |
| Energy products | | 7 |
| Food industry products | | 7 |
| Farm, forestry and fishing products | | 3 |

The goods France imported in 1999 are shown in graph **C**. Some imports like food products are used directly by the people, sometimes called **consumers**. Other imports such as chemicals are used by French industries to make other goods.

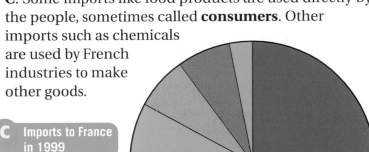

**C** Imports to France in 1999

N

0 _____ 500 km

USA

UK

NETHERLANDS

BELGIUM/ LUXEMBOURG

GERMANY

FRANCE

SWITZERLAND

JAPAN

ITALY

SPAIN

**Key**

 1 mm = 1 %

**D** France's main trading partners for imports in 1999

## Activities

**4 a** Copy the table below, then use pie graph **C** to work out which imports are for consumers, which are used by industry, or both.

**b** Work out the total percentage for each category. **123**

| | Goods | % |
|---|---|---|
| Imports for consumers | | |
| Imports for industry | | |
| Imports for consumers and industry | | |

**5** Compare the figures for exports and imports in graphs **B** and **C**. Make three lists of goods:

- Imports to France greater than exports
- Exports from France greater than imports
- Imports to France similar to exports.

**6** Study map **D**. Write a short paragraph about the countries where France imports most goods from. You should mention:

- The top three importing countries
- The overall pattern of imports
- Any other interesting points you notice.

# France and the European Union

France has economic links with a range of countries. Being part of the European Union means that taxes are not put on goods imported from other EU countries, so these countries form France's major trading partners. France also has trade links with countries that used to be French colonies. Taxes on goods from these countries are usually lower, making them cheaper than goods from other countries.

| | | % of value | | | % of value |
|---|---|---|---|---|---|
| Germany | | 16 | Belgium/ Luxembourg | | 8 |
| UK | | 10 | Netherlands | | 8 |
| Spain | | 9 | Switzerland | | 4 |
| Italy | | 9 | Japan | | 2 |
| USA | | 8 | | | |

**E** France's main trading partners for exports in 1999

## Activities

**7** Draw a map with proportional arrows showing France's main export partners, using the data in table **B**.
- Set your work out like map **D** on page 41.
- Try using this scale for your arrows: 1 mm = 1 per cent of value.

**8** Imagine you work for the French Department of Trade and Industry. It is your job to write a report about trade in France. The title of your report is 'France has a good balance of trade'.

### help!

Use the following structure for your report:

- You will need an introduction to explain what your report is about. Use the following starters and write clear, short sentences:
  - This is a report about …
  - In this report I will cover …
  - These are the issues to be discussed …
  - As a country we have …

- Write a few paragraphs to state who France trades with and describe the patterns of France's international trade. Think about:

  - Who are France's main trading partners?
  - What are the main imports/exports?
  - What is France's balance of trade like?

- Include values and statistics in your report.

- In your conclusion explain why France has a good balance of trade.

# Review and reflect

| | | |
|---|---|---|
| **FRANCE** <br> Europe <br> school | **ENERGY** <br> reserves <br> power | **AGRICULTURE** <br> farming <br> land |
| **PARIS** <br> London <br> capital city | **TECHNOPOLE** <br> Grenoble <br> science park | **THE ALPS** <br> mountains <br> East |

**MANUFACTURING** <br> industry <br> secondary

**TERTIARY** <br> industry <br> high-tech

**NUCLEAR** <br> energy <br> power

**ECONOMY** <br> money <br> country

## Activities

1 In groups of four, read the cards above.

  a Choose one of the cards and describe the word in capitals to the other members of your group *without using any of the other words on the card.*

  b Choose another card and draw a picture to represent the word in capitals.

  c Design some other cards to try out in your group.

2 Add key words and terms you have used to your word bank. You could start with the words on the cards above. 📖

## Learn about

The global fashion industry connects people around the world in different states of development. Interdependence between people, places and environments is increasingly affected by the process of *globalisation*. In this unit you will learn:

- what the global fashion industry is like
- how people, places and environments are connected
- what is meant by *globalisation*
- who takes part in the chain of production and what happens if the chain is broken
- what the future of global fashion might be like.

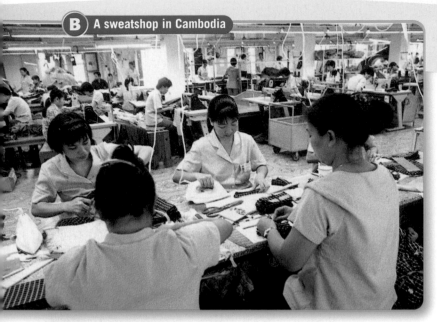

**B** A sweatshop in Cambodia

**C** Catwalk shows help sell fashions

**D** Some views of global fashion

> I don't think workers in the fashion industry are badly treated. Their wages may be low, but it's better than having no job.

> I think clothing workers like us have a right to decent working conditions and pay. I sewed on collars for £4.64 a month. I often worked overtime, without pay. I worked from 7am to 10pm, or sometimes all night.

> Aggressive marketing forces young people to keep up with their friends by buying expensive brand names.

> I like to wear fashionable clothes like the trendy pop stars or sports people. I'm more interested in what the clothes look like than where they come from.

> I don't see why I should buy clothes that create such inequalities for the world's workers. I would rather help to make working conditions fairer.

# Activities

**1** The adverts in **A** show ways in which the fashion industry advertises its products. Take each one in turn and consider these questions.

- What image is the advert trying to create?
- Who is the advert aimed at (the target audience)?
- What slogans are used to persuade people to buy the product?
- What might make you choose this brand over another?
- What don't the advertisements tell you?

**2** Design your own advertisement for a brand of clothing. Think about the slogan and the image/person to use. You could do a poster or a 30-second advert for TV or radio.

**3** The quotes in **D** are things that people might say about aspects of the fashion industry. With a partner, decide how far you agree with the statements by placing them along a **continuum**:

```
1                    5                    10
```
Don't agree                        Completely
at all                                 agree

**4** Think about all the quotes in **D** carefully, then write one to give your own opinion about fashion. You will look back at this at the end of this unit.

**5** Compare the images in photos **B** and **C**. Discuss the differences between them with a partner and look for any issues that might affect the people in them. Make a list and then contribute to a class discussion about the pictures.

**6** Start your word bank of terms for this unit, using the glossary on pages 142–143 to find meanings. Display the key terms as a wall display about global fashion in your classroom.

# Who's the fashion victim?

The fashion industry connects people all around the world. After all, we all wear clothes! Have you ever thought about where your clothes come from, the lives of the people who make them, how the clothes get to you and who shares the money that you paid for them? This unit will investigate all these things and encourage you to explore ideas about the world trade in fashion.

Fashion and clothing – the 'rag trade' – have been economic activities for hundreds of years. **Natural fibres** such as wool or cotton were spun and woven into cloth and then made into garments. In the twentieth century man-made fibres, such as nylon, rayon and polyester, were developed and made into clothes. Today's choice of fabrics and garments in a rainbow of colours, from the most basic item to designer chic, makes the fashion industry one of the most profitable in the world.

## Activities

**1** Look at the labels in your favourite outfit or your school uniform. Find out where each item was made. Note down the *brand name* if there is one, and find out where the company has its headquarters. You could use a search engine to find this information on the Internet. Access the company's website for information about its products. **ICT**

**2** Stick a world map onto the centre of a sheet of A3 paper. Shade in the places where your clothes were made in one colour and the countries where the company headquarters are located in another. You could illustrate your map like the one in **A**.

**3 a** Conduct a class survey. List and tally the places where everyone's clothes were made.

**b** Plot this data by mapping it carefully; you will need to choose an appropriate way of showing how many garments were made in each place. Connect each place to the UK with an arrow.

**4** Now choose a method to present the class data for the location of the headquarters of the companies. **123**

**5** Compare your two class surveys. Is there a difference between the places where the clothes were made and those where the companies are located? Explain your results.

⦿ Where do most clothes/shoes come from?

⦿ Why are clothes/shoes made in so many places?

⦿ Why are they made in some places and not others?

⦿ Why is there a difference between the manufacturing countries and the HQs of the brand-owners?

**6 Extension**
Present the class results on a wall map, using pins of different colours to show where items were made: blue for shirts, green for shoes, etc.

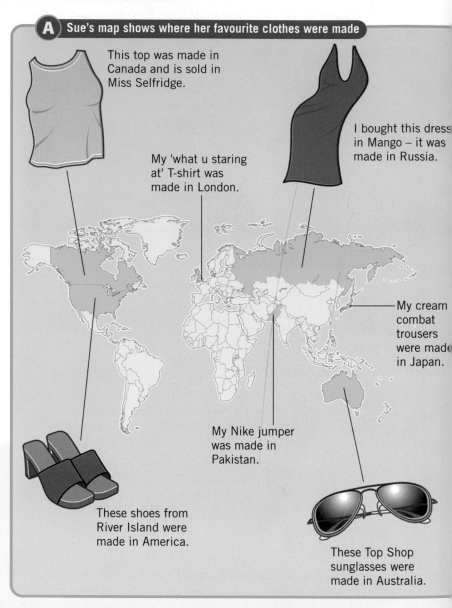

**A** Sue's map shows where her favourite clothes were made

This top was made in Canada and is sold in Miss Selfridge.

My 'what u staring at' T-shirt was made in London.

I bought this dress in Mango – it was made in Russia.

My cream combat trousers were made in Japan.

My Nike jumper was made in Pakistan.

These shoes from River Island were made in America.

These Top Shop sunglasses were made in Australia.

Fashion companies will try to make their products for the cheapest price and with the least trouble. Many companies locate production all over the world, often in poorer countries where the minimum wage is lower. As the needs of a company and the conditions in countries change, the company may move production somewhere else, especially if it is a large organisation or corporation.

Map **B** shows that there are inequalities in the amount of money earned by people in different countries. Development is discussed in more detail in Unit 1 of this book. You may like to read again some of the reasons why inequalities occur and how different places are developing in the world today.

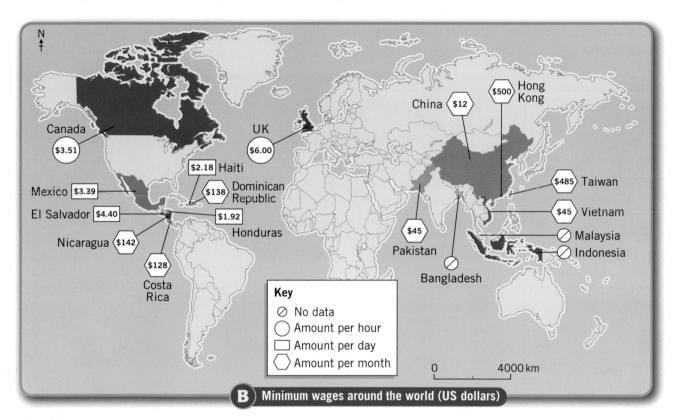

N

Canada $3.51

UK $6.00

China $12

$500 Hong Kong

$2.18 Haiti

Mexico $3.39

$138 Dominican Republic

$485 Taiwan

El Salvador $4.40

$1.92

$45 Vietnam

Nicaragua $142

Honduras

Malaysia

Indonesia

$128

$45

Pakistan

Costa Rica

Bangladesh

**Key**
- ⊘ No data
- ◯ Amount per hour
- ▢ Amount per day
- ⬡ Amount per month

0      4000 km

**B** Minimum wages around the world (US dollars)

## Activities

**7** Map **B** shows minimum wage data for selected countries around the world.

**a** First, calculate the *minimum wage per month* for the countries which have data per day or per hour. Use a 40-hour week as a guide.

**b** List all the places in rank order and draw a graph to show the results. Write about your graph – what do the results show?

**c** Add the minimum wage per month information to the class survey map from activity **3**. You will need to find out the data for any countries not listed.

**d** Use the maps on page 12 or the Internet to find the GNP (Gross National Product) and HDI (Human Development Index) of the places you have plotted on your map.

**e** Now compare all your data from the activities on these two pages and write it up as a report to the United Nations about the state of global fashion, using the title *Who's the fashion victim?* Use these headings:

- ⑥ Where fashion items are made
- ⑥ Pay rates around the world
- ⑥ Who's the victim? 📖

**8** **Extension**

Use the Internet to find more information about the global fashion industry. For example, you could investigate the foreign debt of the places on your map. You can find useful links at www.heinemann.co.uk/hotlinks

# Global fashion links

The poet John Donne wrote that 'No man is an island', and the same is true of countries. Countries everywhere are **interdependent** – they rely upon other places for trade or **commodities** to keep their economies going. Some places have been linked together for many years, while others are relatively new **trading partners**. Who are the key players around the globe in the fashion industry and what parts do they play in the process?

## The fashion industry – chains of production

The fashion industry involves millions of people each day. From the people who grow cotton to shop assistants on the High Street, everyone has an important part to play in the chain of production.

PAKISTAN — *farmer*
INDIA — *factory worker*
INDIA — *factory manager*
USA — *brand owner*
UK — *retailer*
UK — *consumer*

## Activities

**A** Cotton – from plant to person

① Drawings **A** and **B** show the chain of production for a T-shirt. Plot the people and their locations on a world map, connecting them with arrows. Discuss these questions as a group:

   ⊚ How many places are connected?

   ⊚ Who has power in the chain? Explain what you think.

   ⊚ Are there winners and losers? If so, who?

② The people in different parts of the production chain are shown in **B**. Divide your class into six groups that take on one role each. Discuss the answers to these questions in your group, then feed back to the class:

   ⊚ Who is this person?

   ⊚ Who do they work for?

   ⊚ How are they linked in the chain?

   ⊚ What is their life like?

   ⊚ Who makes their decisions?

③ If the people in the chain are all involved in the production of a garment which costs US $100, decide as a group how much each person should get as their share.

   Make sure that you can justify your reasons.

④ Reorganise into new groups that each contain a representative from each person in the chain. Compare your shares and write a short report bringing together what you decided in your old groups.

# Farmer

- The farmer works seven days a week to produce the cotton for the factories.
- The farmer must grow good quality cotton. Any spare money is invested in improving the land, so the farmer is often in debt.
- In a good year the profit made from selling the crop is good, but when the weather is poor the farmer's family may go hungry.
- The farmer's life is unpredictable. The dream of the small farmer is to be sure of a buyer for the crop.

# Manufacturer

- The manufacturer produces goods for the brand-owner.
- To stay in business, he must charge the brand-owner as little as possible.
- Low profits mean little money to improve factory conditions.
- The manufacturer tries to keep to the Code of Practice for health and safety in the factory, but inspections are rare.
- The manufacturer allows workers to join trade unions but sacks trouble-makers.

# Retailer

- The retailer sells the product to the public and takes a large share of the price – about £23 from a £50 garment.
- The retailer buys goods from the brand-owners at the lowest possible price to maximise profits.
- The retailer likes to buy 'brand named' goods because they can be sold for higher prices.

# Consumer

- The consumer buys the product from the retailer in the high street.
- The consumer wants to pay a low price for the product, but will pay more for quality goods with a brand name.
- The consumer is concerned about poor conditions in factories in LEDCs. Countries have taken out loans to provide basic needs for their people, but poverty is still an issue.

# Factory worker

- The factory worker works for twelve hours a day, six days a week. The factory is cramped, dark and dusty, and workers are often badly treated.
- The pay is only 60p an hour, hardly enough to live on, but jobs in the city are scarce.
- The factory worker often has to do overtime. The work is very tiring and there is no time off for illness. Pregnant women are sacked.
- The factory worker has joined a trade union, but it doesn't seem to have made any difference.

# Brand-owner

- The brand-owner wants to be the world market leader to make as much money as possible.
- To keep production costs down they locate in countries that pay low wages for factory work.
- The brand-owner has a Code of Practice to protect the factory workers from poor working conditions.
- The brand-owner will pay famous people large amounts of money to endorse their product.
- The company has an annual turnover of £2.4bn and makes a profit of £190 million.

## Activities

5. **a** Hold a class debate to explore the decisions you made.

   **b** Next, look at **E** on page 50 to see how the money is divided in real life.

   **c** Now write a newspaper article, using the role play as your focus.

6. Convert the figures in **E** on page 50 from dollars into pounds using the current exchange rate. Comment on the shares between the people in the chain.

The information on these two pages focuses on the people at the start of the production process – the factory workers. Many garments and shoes are made in developing countries (LEDCs). Here labour is cheaper and factory overheads are lower, so the brand-owners can make bigger profits.

Life in these factories has been well publicised in the media and many have been called 'sweatshops'. For example, in 2000 a documentary in the BBC Panorama series exposed factories who were producing goods for Gap and Nike, and challenged some of the working practices in Cambodia.

# Adidas attacked for Asian 'sweatshops'

**D** Taken from an article by Andrew Osborn, *The Guardian*, 23 November 2000

Indonesian factory workers producing clothes for German sportswear giant Adidas are subject to forced overtime, physical abuse and poverty-line wages, the European parliament was told yesterday.

In a controversial hearing organised by a British MEP, Richard Howitt, an Indonesian non-governmental organisation described how workers toiled in Dickensian conditions which, it said, breached the company's own code of conduct. 'Wages are still below the legal minimum set by the government, the number of hours people work exceeds the legal maximum and people are paid less than a dollar a day,' said Rainy Hutarabat of Urban Community Mission after the hearing, which Adidas did not attend. Underpayment and poor conditions for child workers are not confined to Indonesia. The problem is severe in India where, according to aid organisations, children are making sports goods in appalling conditions. The new allegations against Adidas centre on the Tuntex factory in Jakarta, where 1700 workers, most of them women, produce jackets and socks.

# Gap and Nike: No sweat?

*Panorama* reveals that Gap and Nike have been using a factory in Cambodia that breaks their own strict codes of conduct and anti-sweatshop rules.

The two hugely successful international brands claim that regular monitoring ensures that most factories are free of unacceptable working practices. However, the *Panorama* team uncovered sweatshop working conditions and child labour at the June Textiles factory in Cambodia.

Sun Thyda, 12, lied about her age to get the job. She says: 'I didn't want to come here, but we're very poor so I had to come.'

Six other girls spoke about their working conditions. All work seven days a week, often up to 16 hours a day.

Nike and Gap told *Panorama* that they are working with the factory to improve conditions. Nike may even stop using the factory altogether in December.

**E** Fair shares?

- Paid to the factory: 12 per cent
- Profit: 2 per cent
- Production costs: 2 per cent
- Material: 7.6 per cent
- Wages: 0.4 per cent

US $100

- Brand-owner: 33 per cent
- Research: 11 per cent
- Store: 50 per cent
- Publicity: 8.5 per cent
- Profit: 13.5 per cent
- Transport costs: 5 per cent

# My job

### What is your job?
I make clothing for American companies.

### Where do you work?
In a factory in Tehuacàn, Mexico.

### How many hours do you work each week?
We all work from 8 am to 7 pm, Monday to Friday. If any work is rejected, we may stay until 10 pm. On Saturdays we work from 8 am to 2 pm, but we often don't leave until 4 pm. We don't get breaks, not even to eat.

### How much money do you earn?
US $28 a week.

### What do you pay for with your salary?
Food, housing, clothes, transport and other essentials.

### Do you ever have money left over?
No. The government says that enough food for my family costs about US $70 a week. That's without housing and the other things we have to buy.

### Do you get benefits?   No.

### Can you get promotion?   No.

### Do you work at the weekend?
Yes, always Saturday, sometimes Sunday.

### Where do you eat lunch?   On the street.

### What kind of relationship do you have with your boss?   He yells at me and shoves me.

### What happens if you arrive late for work?
They take 10 pesos from our pay if we're five minutes late. Sometimes they won't let us into the factory until 9 am – they take away 30 pesos for that.

### Are you paid if you work overtime?   No.

### How much holiday do you get?
We can take a week off at Christmas, but we have to make it up by working on Sundays.

### Can you join a union?   No.

### Are you punished for staying home if you are sick?   Yes.

### Do people who do a dangerous job get protective equipment?   No.

### How many times can you go to the toilet at work each day?   The supervisor gets mad if we go more than once.

## Activities

7  Look at the information on these two pages, then do some research to find out more about working conditions in parts of the developing world. You can find useful website links at www.heinemann.co.uk/hotlinks

Present your findings as a poster; think of a catchy headline and use a desktop publishing program for a really professional finish. **ICT**

8  Look at the questionnaire in **F**. Ask a relative or friend who has a job to answer the same questions, then compare your findings with **F** and present them to the class. Produce a display to compare UK jobs with those in developing countries.

9  Check that you have all the words in bold type in your word bank. Add them to the class display if you have one.

# What happens when the chain of production is broken?

## Case Study: Kukdong factory, Mexico

*In January 2001 the 800 workers at the Kukdong factory in Atlixco, Mexico went on strike to protest at the working conditions in their factory. Kukdong International is a Korean-based producer with branches in Indonesia, Brazil and Mexico. The factory produces goods for Nike, Reebok and many US universities.*

*The strike began on Tuesday January 9 – read how the story unfolded, as reported on the Internet by the Clean Clothes Campaign and by Nike using the links at www.heinemann.co.uk/hotlinks.*

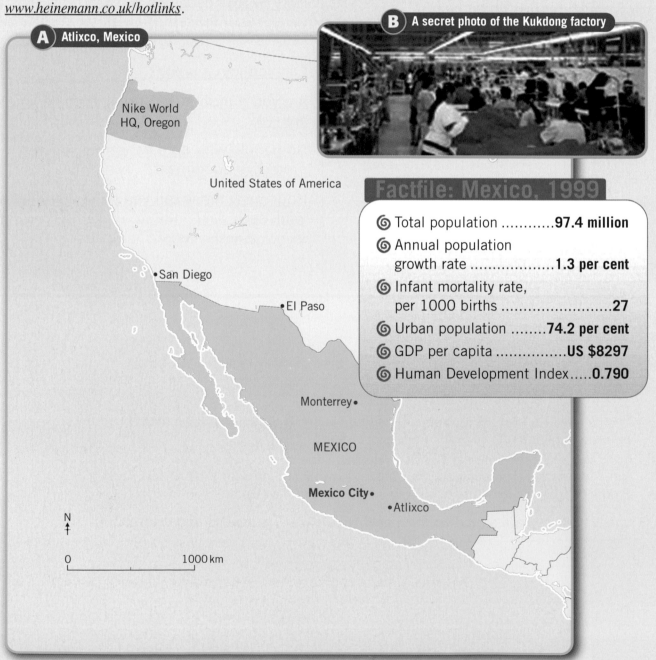

**A** Atlixco, Mexico

Nike World HQ, Oregon

United States of America

• San Diego

• El Paso

Monterrey •

MEXICO

Mexico City •

• Atlixco

N

0          1000 km

**B** A secret photo of the Kukdong factory

### Factfile: Mexico, 1999

- Total population ............**97.4 million**
- Annual population growth rate ...................**1.3 per cent**
- Infant mortality rate, per 1000 births .........................**27**
- Urban population ........**74.2 per cent**
- GDP per capita ...............**US $8297**
- Human Development Index.....**0.790**

All 800 workers go on strike to protest at unjust sackings and other abuses of workers' rights in the factory.

<u>The workers demand that:</u>

1  All workers return to work, including the sacked workers.
2  The company agrees not to fire or punish anyone for taking part in the strike.
3  The company recognises the Kukdong Workers' Coalition as the Union for the workers and agrees to negotiate with them.

The workers plan to continue the strike until the company meets their demands. Police in full riot gear attack 300 workers who were guarding the factory gates.

The company agrees to allow the workers to come back to work without anyone being punished.

The workers try to return to work but they are locked out and told that they are fired.

The clothing companies and the factory management agree that the factory should be inspected. An independent monitoring company, Verite, was chosen, which was accredited by the Fair Labour Association (FLA). It was asked to write a report both to the FLA and to the companies involved.

The inspectors begin their five-day visit. They use the same standards as in many other countries throughout the world.

**March**
**13**
2001

More than 500 of the 800 workers return to work. Nike, Reebok and Kukdong management are working closely with local government officials and NGOs to help workers return to their jobs at Kukdong without punishment. They help the factory management to make changes, based on the inspectors' report. The improvement plan and Verite's report can be found at Nike's website through www.heinemann.co.uk/hotlinks

**March**
**18**
2001

The Kukdong workers meet to form an independent trade union.

**March**
**27**
2001

Reports from Mexico say that the atmosphere in the Kukdong plant is calmer than it has been in months. The leaders of the independent union are investigating workers' grievances and meeting with management on their behalf.

The next step is the legal recognition of the union in Mexico, which should allow fairer working practices in the Kukdong factory in Atlixco.

'Our first priority was to stabilise the factory, working with an independent labour expert. After 500 workers returned to work, we next sought to ensure the rights of the workers were being respected.'

'Nike is committed to taking action to ensure that Kukdong provides a fair, safe and healthy environment for the men and women working there. Nike will also continue to hold Kukdong to the standards outlined in Nike's Code of Conduct to strengthen our commitment to long-term improvement for workers making Nike products around the world.'

*Dusty Kidd, Vice-President for corporate responsibility, Nike*

File      Edit      View      Go      Favourite    Help      Back      Forward    Stop

Address:    http://www.

Search

Check e-mail     Finance     Help

**C**   **Photos from the Nike website show lunch, the embroidery room and free transport**

# Activities

1. Read about the strike at the Kukdong factory. Take the role of the workers, the factory-owners and Nike in turn and summarise the cause of the strike from their point of view in no more than 20 words for each viewpoint.

2. Discuss the issues raised by the strike and make some comments under these headings to include in a debate about fair working practices in factories:
   - Factory workers' rights
   - Membership of a union
   - Factory-owner's opinion
   - Role of the brand-owners (Nike, Reebok, etc.)
   - How consumers can help.

3. Consider the effect that the strike had on the people in each part of the chain of production. Using the groups that you were in for activity **2** on page 49, discuss the impact on you and then share your ideas by taping an interview or writing a report for a newspaper about the strike.

4. Think of other ways that the chain of production might be broken. Make a list of these ways and write down how you think that each problem could be resolved. Set it out as a table like the one below.

| Problem | Solution |
| --- | --- |
|  |  |
|  |  |

# Globalisation – what is it and what drives it?

Everyone in the world is becoming more and more connected together. Many of the clothes and shoes you wear were made by people thousands of miles away. Jobs in the UK, as well as in the countries where these clothes are produced, depend upon trade with or investment in faraway places. People travel more, money flows around the world with the push of a button, and the World Wide Web makes it easier than ever before to connect and keep in touch. This process is called *globalisation*.

As you saw in Unit 1, the UK government has made a pledge to make globalisation work for everyone. The Government White Paper on international development sets targets for international development for completion by 2015.

Globalisation has been speeded up by large companies who can afford to locate all over the world, usually searching for bigger markets and higher profits. They are called **transnational corporations** (TNCs) and include Ford, Coca Cola, General Motors, Shell, IBM, Unilever, Sony and Nestlé. Major TNCs in the fashion industry include sportswear giants like Nike, Reebok and Adidas, and companies such as Gap, Levi Strauss and H&M. These brand names are recognised the world over and their logos are among the most widely recognised images on the planet. The annual incomes of the leading ten TNCs are shown in table **A**. For comparison, the annual incomes (GDP) of ten selected countries are shown in **B**.

> 'The world is SMALLER than it has ever been. Its six billion citizens are CLOSER to each other than ever before in history.'
>
> **UK Department for International Development (DFID) 2000**

**B** GDP of ten selected countries (billions of US dollars)

| Country | GDP |
|---------|-----|
| Bangladesh | 46.0 |
| Chile | 67.5 |
| Indonesia | 142.5 |
| Ireland | 93.4 |
| Israel | 100.8 |
| Norway | 152.9 |
| Portugal | 113.7 |
| Saudia Arabia | 139.4 |
| Singapore | 84.9 |
| Switzerland | 258.6 |

*Data for 1999 from UNDP website*

| Corporation | Annual income |
|-------------|---------------|
| Exxon Mobil (USA) | 232.75 |
| Walmart (USA) | 191.33 |
| General Motors (USA) | 178.76 |
| Ford Motor Company (USA) | 170.06 |
| Daimler Chrysler (Germany/USA) | 152.11 |
| Royal Dutch Shell (Netherlands/UK) | 149.15 |
| BP (UK) | 148.06 |
| General Electric (USA) | 129.85 |
| Toyota Motor Company (Japan) | 112.94 |
| Mitsubishi (Japan) | 110.33 |

**A** Annual income of the ten largest TNCs (billions of US dollars)

*Data for 2000 from Fortune website*

Supporters of globalisation argue that TNCs bring jobs and new technology to the developing nations of the world. Critics of globalisation say they have become too powerful and that they control the global economy. Some TNCs are wealthier and more powerful than many countries. Of the world's richest 100 economies, 49 are countries and 51 are TNCs.

## Activities

1 Look at tables **A** and **B**, which show the amount of money made by some corporations and countries. Draw a new table which merges the data from both tables into rank order, from the highest to the lowest. (123)

2 Describe what your new table shows, looking carefully at the nearest neighbour to each TNC in terms of wealth.

3 Plot the countries and TNC headquarters on to a world map to show their locations. Describe what the map shows. Is there a 'power base' from the data you have been given? Look for the most powerful places in the world. Does the data surprise you?

4 Look back at the countries you plotted on your world map to show where your clothes were made (page 46, activity **2**). Find out their GNPs and compare them to the companies shown in the table. What do you notice?

5 Find out about the annual income for a company of your choice. Use a search engine to do this, or look up www.heinemann.co.uk/hotlinks to find a list of company profiles through Yahoo! Finance. Add this company to the table that you drew for activity **1**. (ICT)

6 Present your findings in a short report to the class about the company using the Development Compass Rose below as your guide. Display your company information as a poster, too.

**Natural**
• Which resources does it use (local/distant)?
• What are the impacts on the environment (local/regional/global/local elsewhere)?

**Who decides?**
• Where are the decision-makers located?
• Who has control over the process?
• What is the impact on/of local/national democratic processes?

**Where is the company located:**
• HQ?
• branch plants?

**Economic**
• What are the positive/negative economic effects (local/national/local elsewhere)?
• Who gains? Who loses?
• Where are these located?

**Social**
• What are the cultural impacts?
• Who gains? Who loses?
• What is the social impact?
• Where are the winners and losers located in society?

# Fair trade in fashion?

The fashion industry is a global economic activity with complex links between people who may be thousands of miles apart. It is a difficult task to ensure that working conditions are the same the world over. Many transnational companies have Codes of Conduct and monitoring procedures to ensure that production of clothing occurs in a way that ensures fair trade for all.

During the 1970s and 1980s, more and more TNCs used subcontractors (other companies) to produce their goods. A well known example is Nike. They employ 5000 people directly, but a further 600 000 workers are employed by smaller companies who produce clothes and shoes for Nike.

The International Labour Organisation, which is part of the United Nations, has developed international labour standards. Companies like Nike use these to draw up Codes of Conduct for their factories.

## Activities

1. In pairs, discuss what you think should be included in a Code of Conduct for workers in factories producing clothing or shoes. Look at the 'My job' questionnaire on page 51 to help you think about the working conditions in some factories. Present this as a poster which could be displayed in the workplace.

2. Compare your code of conduct with one that you have researched from the Internet. Choose a well known company and use a search engine like Lycos, Yahoo! or Google to search for the information. Start with a general search for the clothing company, then use their website to find their Code of Conduct. (ICT)

3. Design a fair trade T-shirt which highlights the issues in global fashion today.

# Review and reflect

## What is the future for fashion?

In an increasingly globalised world, where people and places are connected more closely than ever before, what does the future hold? People will always need clothes, but how will the production of those items change and develop? Will trade unions and demands for workers' rights be a powerful force, or will the transnational companies continue to dominate world markets with their influence over production bases in less developed countries?

## Activities

1. Read through all the work you have completed, then look through Unit 3 again. Look back at your opinion about fashion from question **4** on page 45, and decide whether your opinion on global fashion has changed. Think about:

   ⊚ the winners and losers in the process

   ⊚ who benefits from the fashion trade

   ⊚ how people and places are connected.

   Present your own views about globalisation of the fashion industry and world trade in a piece of persuasive writing. Design this as a flyer for distribution to young people and share it with the class in a final discussion.

2. Complete a crystal ball exercise. Look into the future, twenty years from now. What might the fashion industry be like then, and why? You might like to think about *expected* and *preferred* futures. Write up and explain your predictions to the class.

# 4 Tourism – good or bad?

## What is tourism?

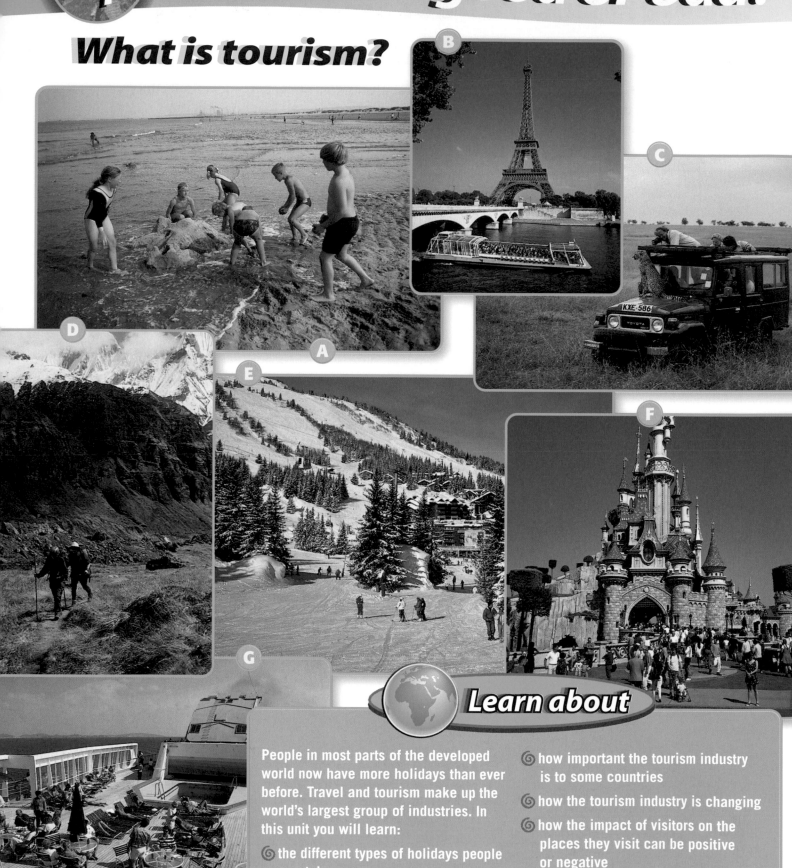

## Learn about

People in most parts of the developed world now have more holidays than ever before. Travel and tourism make up the world's largest group of industries. In this unit you will learn:

- the different types of holidays people can take
- what jobs are provided by the tourism industry
- how important the tourism industry is to some countries
- how the tourism industry is changing
- how the impact of visitors on the places they visit can be positive or negative
- how tourism can be more sustainable.

# How important is tourism as an economic activity?

## Activities

**1** **a** With a partner, look at photographs **A** to **G** and make a list of all the different types of holiday they show. Add as many others as you can think of.

**b** How many different groups or headings can you fit those types of holiday in to?

**2** **a** For each photograph, make a list of all the attractions of that area.

**b** Identify whether these attractions are physical/natural (e.g. snow in photograph **E**), or human (e.g. the Eiffel Tower in photograph **B**).

**3** Choose one photograph of a place you would like to visit. Can you think of any negative impacts people might have on the area in the photograph you have chosen?

**4** Look at all the photographs on page 60. List all the jobs that will be created by the types of holidays that you can see. Start from the moment they are advertised on TV. Classify the jobs according to their type, as shown in the table below.

| Primary sector jobs | Secondary sector jobs | Tertiary sector jobs |
|---|---|---|
| Farmers to supply food to hotels | Construction worker at hotel | Travel agent |
|  |  |  |

**5** Shade all the jobs which you think will be seasonal, i.e. only available at certain times of the year. Explain why this is the case.

**6** Copy and complete a large version of the Venn diagram on the right by writing each job in the correct section.

Summer        Winter

Both

# How and why is the tourism industry changing?

Tourism is a constantly changing industry. Many things influence where people choose to go on holiday. For example, some people like to go to familiar places, others are looking for somewhere different. There are also fashions for different types of holidays and, of course, for most people price is important. Many holiday resorts have gone through a period of growth followed by a period of decline as people change their choice of holiday. The graphs and tables on these pages show some of the changing patterns of holidays taken by people from the UK and some reasons for those patterns.

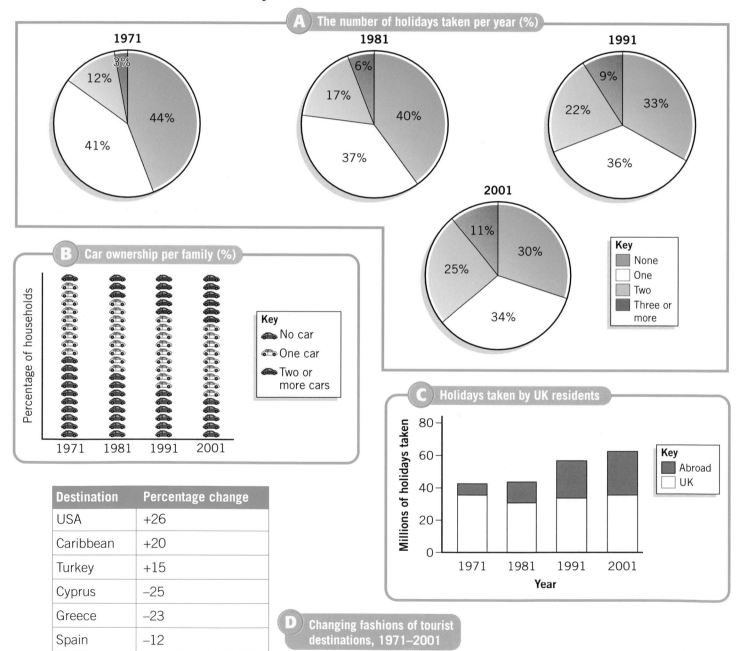

**A** The number of holidays taken per year (%)

1971 · 1981 · 1991 · 2001

Key — None · One · Two · Three or more

**B** Car ownership per family (%)

Key — No car · One car · Two or more cars

Percentage of households — 1971 · 1981 · 1991 · 2001

**C** Holidays taken by UK residents

Millions of holidays taken — 1971 · 1981 · 1991 · 2001 — Year

Key — Abroad · UK

| Destination | Percentage change |
|---|---|
| USA | +26 |
| Caribbean | +20 |
| Turkey | +15 |
| Cyprus | −25 |
| Greece | −23 |
| Spain | −12 |

**D** Changing fashions of tourist destinations, 1971–2001

**E** Top ten tourist destinations for UK visitors, 2000

## Blackpool to Benidorm

- On the first post-war Saturday of July 1945, trains carried a record 102 890 trippers to Blackpool. Beaches had been off-limits since the start of the war.

- The Holiday with Pay Act turned this weekend exodus into a two-week annual adventure for workers.

- The working class went to Blackpool or Margate. The middle classes preferred the more select beaches of Bournemouth and Eastbourne.

- In the summer of 1948 there were almost 8000 cases of polio in Britain. Many were blamed on the polluted beaches around Britain's coast.

- In 1948 one in 20 British holidaymakers went to a Butlin's holiday camp for their holidays.

- By the 1960s millions of Britons were creating Margates and Brightons on the Mediterranean Sea and in 1970 5.7 million British people chose to go to Spain on holiday, mostly through package tours.

- By 2000, 40 per cent of all holidays taken by Britons were spent abroad.

**F** Adapted from *The Guardian*, July 1999

## Activities

**1** Copy and complete the following paragraphs:

Since 1971 the number of holidays taken by residents of Great Britain has increased from _____ million to _____ million. An increasing proportion of these have been taken abroad and by 2001 _____ per cent of holidays were taken outside Great Britain.

Reasons for the increase in holidays might include the fact that more people own cars. In 1971 _____ million families had no car, but by 2001 this figure had decreased to _____ million. The increase in the number of motorways has also made resorts more accessible.

In 1971, 56 per cent of the population took at least one holiday. By 2001 this had risen to _____ per cent. This is because _____ .

The introduction of the package holiday meant that it was easy to travel abroad, and in 2000 the three most popular holiday destinations for Britons were _____ , _____ and _____ .

**2** Prepare a report for the British Tourist Authority on the main changes and trends in the tourism industry in the UK since 1971. Include sections on:
- the total demand for holidays
- the types of holidays people choose to go on
- the destinations of the holidaymakers
- how you think that the holiday industry may change in the future.

**a** Begin each section of the report with an enquiry question. For example, the first paragraph could start with: 'How has the demand for holidays changed and what are the reasons for this?'

**b** Include in your report graphs, diagrams, maps and pictures.

**3** **Extension**

You may wish to make a database and generate your graphs using a computer. More information is available from tourism websites (see www.heinemann.co.uk/hotlinks for suggestions). ICT

## Case Study

# What is the impact of the tourist industry in Blackpool and St Lucia?

## Blackpool

Blackpool is a typical British seaside resort. The coming of the railway in 1846 made Blackpool a busy, popular holiday destination as it was within an hour's ride of the dirty, smoky cotton towns of Manchester, Bolton and Rochdale. For many of the mill workers, the highlight of the year was the works' outing to Blackpool. With the arrival of cars and coaches, Blackpool continued to grow and today 16 million people visit the town each year.

⊚ There are 11 km of wide sandy beach backed by a promenade where people like to walk and take the sea air.

⊚ Lining the promenade are the more expensive hotels where guests pay more to overlook the sea.

⊚ The major tourist attractions can also be found in this zone, such as Blackpool Tower, the piers and the famous Pleasure Beach.

⊚ In the zone behind the sea front are the cheaper hotels and guest houses, and Blackpool's CBD (Central Business District), which contains the main shopping area and offices.

⊚ The train station and bus station are also in this area so that people do not have to walk far to reach the beach or the other attractions.

⊚ Furthest away from the sea are the residential areas, parks and other areas of commercial land use, such as the business park.

**A**

# The Illuminations ...............

First installed in 1879, the lights stretch for about nine kilometres along the sea front. They attract 8 million visitors a year and shine for 66 nights, extending the season by nine weeks at a time when most other resorts have closed down.

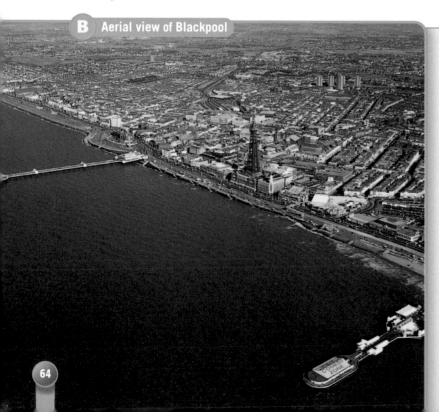
**B** Aerial view of Blackpool

Blackpool's heyday as a holiday destination for the British annual family holiday is long gone. The number of visitors staying and spending money in Blackpool has fallen in the past 30 years as people go abroad for better weather. People are changing not only their holiday destinations, but also the types of holidays they take. Far more holidaymakers camp, climb, visit rainforests and theme parks, or travel long distances than ever before.

The government has set up tourist boards in England, Wales, Scotland and Northern Ireland to give advice to businesses and to provide information for tourists. Resorts are encouraged to adapt to the changing demand for short breaks, day trips and special interest holidays, and cash for improvements is available from the National Lottery.

**D** Blackpool's climate

**E** Britain's main seaside holiday resorts

**C** Extract from an OS map of Blackpool, scale 1: 25 000

| Home address | % | Home address | % |
|---|---|---|---|
| Lancashire | 17 | Cheshire | 4 |
| Scotland | 15 | Greater Manchester | 4 |
| Yorkshire and Humberside | 13 | Merseyside | 4 |
| | | South West | 4 |
| West Midlands | 9 | East Midlands | 3 |
| Wales | 6 | Greater London | 3 |
| South East | 6 | Derbyshire | 3 |
| North East | 6 | Other | 3 |

**F** Home addresses of visitor to Blackpool, July 2000

## Activities

**1** Write a paragraph to explain why Blackpool has declined as a popular destination for holidaymakers.

**2** Make a list of all the ways that Blackpool tries to extend its season to provide more work.

**3** Use photograph **B** to draw a sketch map of the land use zones in Blackpool. Use map **C** to help you. Use one colour to label the natural attractions (for example, the sea) and another colour to label the human attractions (for example, the Tower).

**4** You can find out more about Blackpool on the Internet. Visit www.heinemann.co.uk/hotlinks.

**help!**

Think about climate, attractions and alternative destinations.

# St Lucia

St Lucia is an island of 616 km² in the Windward Islands chain, 160 km due west of Barbados. The capital city of Castries and the surrounding villages in the north are home to 40 per cent of the island's population and these are also the most popular tourist areas.

Until recently the main income for the islanders has come from growing and exporting bananas. Today, however, the island receives as much income from tourism as it does from the traditional cash crop. Although the St Lucians realise the importance of tourism to their country, they are working hard to avoid ruining their land with overbuilding. The island is also diversifying its agricultural base, which strengthens its economy further by reducing imports. Other cash crops include mangoes, tomatoes, limes and oranges.

**A** St Lucia, a tropical paradise

**B** The location of St Lucia

**Castries**
St Lucia's bustling capital is home to several of the island's historic sights. There is excellent shopping in the town's market.

**Gros Islet**
This village comes alive for the Friday night jazz street parties.

**East coast**
The east coast road twists and turns through many villages, passing many banana and coconut plantations.

**Canaries**
An afternoon's visit to this tiny fishing village offers an interesting study of one of St Lucia's main traditions – fishing in dugout canoes.

**Rainforest**
The central part of the island is covered in rainforest, where wild orchids, giant ferns and birds of paradise flourish, including the indigenous and rare St Lucia parrot.

**Les Pitons**
The south is dominated by Les Pitons, the island's unusual twin peaks which rise from the sea to more than 800 metres. Nearby reefs are an attraction for divers.

**Soufrière**
Located in the south, Soufrière is the oldest town in St Lucia, having been established by the French in 1746. Nearby are the famous volcanic springs – a major tourist attraction.

**Choiseul**
The village of Choiseul is rich in history and crafts, and has some spectacular views.

**Key**
- Main holiday areas
- ▲ Upland areas

# ♥ *Weddings and honeymoons in St Lucia*

*St Lucia, known for its lush tropical beauty and breathtaking scenery, is highly regarded as a romantic treat and a honeymoon and wedding destination. Most of the hotels in St Lucia provide special facilities for couples getting married on the island; some will also provide a private room or suite for the ceremony, if you prefer.*

**D**

## ST LUCIA MIRROR

### WATER SHORTAGE

Hotel owners warn that water rationing will affect trade.

**E** Adapted from a newspaper article

### BRITISH FOREIGN OFFICE ADVICE TO VISITORS

*Last Updated: 11 May 2001*

Most visits to St Lucia are trouble-free, but visitors should be aware that crime is on the increase and muggings can occur at any time, day or night. Visitors should not become complacent because of the friendly, laid-back nature of the island.

**F** Advice to visitors

| Average number of rainy days per month | Month | Average maximum daily temperature (°C) |
|---|---|---|
| 18 | January | 28 |
| 13 | February | 28 |
| 13 | March | 29 |
| 10 | April | 31 |
| 16 | May | 31 |
| 21 | June | 31 |
| 23 | July | 31 |
| 22 | August | 31 |
| 21 | September | 31 |
| 19 | October | 31 |
| 20 | November | 29 |
| 19 | December | 28 |

**G** St Lucia's climate

**H** Origins of tourists to St Lucia in 1999

## Activities

**1** Draw a sketch map of St Lucia and annotate it with the attractions of the island for a holidaymaker. Use one colour to label the natural attractions (for example, Les Pitons) and another colour to label the human attractions (for example, the market at Castries).

**2** Use table **G** to draw a climate graph for St Lucia. **123**

**3** Choose either Blackpool or St Lucia and carry out an enquiry to answer the following question:

> Is Blackpool/St Lucia a successful tourist destination?

**a** More information can be found by clicking on www.heinemann.co.uk/hotlinks for St Lucia websites.

**b** Write up your work as a poster which can be displayed to show the good and bad points of tourism in your chosen resort. You could use a desktop publishing program to produce this. **ICT**

**4** Write a five-minute script for a television holiday programme which compares Blackpool and St Lucia. Use the following headings:

◎ What is the resort like?

◎ What does it offer visitors? (Think about natural and human attractions.)

◎ Who goes there and where are they from?

◎ How and why does the resort benefit or suffer from the tourism industry? (Classify these into social, economic and environmental effects.)

# How can tourism be more sustainable?

Many developing countries are becoming popular tourist destinations. Tourism can bring many benefits, such as jobs. It can also result in costs, such as pollution or environmental damage. People in these countries are also made more aware of the inequalities between themselves and the visitors in terms of their quality of life. Visitors can sometimes offend the local people by the way they dress or the lack of respect they show for local customs and religion.

The key is to minimise the damage – to strike a balance so that holidaymakers can enjoy themselves without destroying what attracted them in the first place. This type of tourism is known as **sustainable tourism** or **ecotourism** and is relevant to all places, whether they are seaside resorts, urban areas or countryside in developing or developed countries. Sustainable tourism also means making sure that local people benefit from the industry, not just big tour companies. For example, local people need to be involved in making decisions which affect their lives.

**A** Adapted from an extract in *Holiday Which?*, Spring 1999

## How to be an ecotourist

### Before you go
- Get rid of unnecessary packaging and swap plastic for paper.
- Try to take eco-friendly shampoos and sun lotions.

### While you're away
- Get out and be adventurous – if you always stay in the hotel, little money will filter through to local people.
- Try local dishes and drinks instead of sticking to imported brands.

### In the hotel
- Don't waste energy. Turn off the lights and air-conditioning when you leave your room.
- Don't waste water.

### Out and about
- Consider using public transport or hire a bicycle to get around.
- Buy presents and souvenirs from local craftspeople and pay a fair price.
- Ask permission before photographing people.
- Dress appropriately – don't offend local people. Remember you are a guest in their country.

## Activities

1. Write a sentence to explain what is meant by sustainable tourism.

2. Copy and complete the table to show how five suggestions in box **A** encourage sustainable tourism. One example has been completed for you.

| Suggestion | Reason(s) |
|---|---|
| Get rid of unnecessary packaging | Host country does not have to burn or bury additional waste |
|  |  |

# Review and reflect

## What are the effects of tourism?

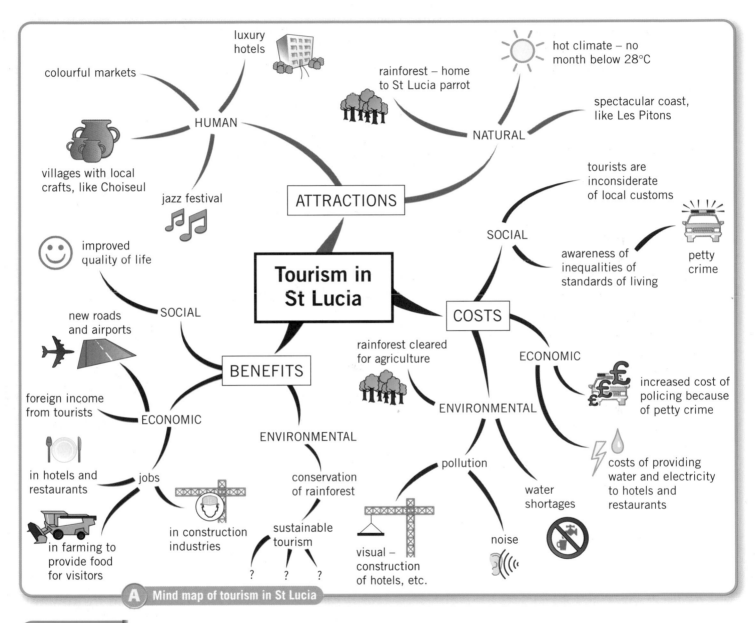

luxury hotels

colourful markets

HUMAN

rainforest – home to St Lucia parrot

hot climate – no month below 28°C

spectacular coast, like Les Pitons

NATURAL

villages with local crafts, like Choiseul

jazz festival

**ATTRACTIONS**

tourists are inconsiderate of local customs

SOCIAL

improved quality of life

**Tourism in St Lucia**

awareness of inequalities of standards of living

petty crime

new roads and airports

SOCIAL

**COSTS**

foreign income from tourists

**BENEFITS**

rainforest cleared for agriculture

ECONOMIC

increased cost of policing because of petty crime

ECONOMIC

ENVIRONMENTAL

in hotels and restaurants

ENVIRONMENTAL

pollution

water shortages

costs of providing water and electricity to hotels and restaurants

jobs

conservation of rainforest

in farming to provide food for visitors

in construction industries

sustainable tourism

? ? ?

visual – construction of hotels, etc.

noise

**A**   Mind map of tourism in St Lucia

## Activities

**1**   **a**   Look carefully at the mind map above. It shows information about the tourism industry in St Lucia – an economically less developed country. Use it as a model to draw a similar mind map for a holiday resort in the United Kingdom, or another more economically developed country of your choice.

  **b**   Collect some holiday brochures and use information from pages 61 to 68 here to help investigate them. If you are able to, add facts from research you have carried out on the Internet. ICT

  **c**   Try to expand your mind map to include ways in which tourism at your chosen resort could become more sustainable.

**2**   Add the key words from this unit to your word bank.

# 5 Comparing countries

## What do we do when we compare countries?

Comparing two or more countries means studying the countries side by side to see how far they are similar and how far they are different. By comparing two countries we will end up with a much better understanding of both countries.

日本

**B** Japan

中国

**A** China, the Middle Kingdom

**C**

**D**

## Learn about

What is it really like to live in another country? Every country is different, but why are countries different? Why do parts of some countries seem very familiar? Finding out about and comparing places is an important geographical skill. In this unit you will learn:

⊚ about two countries in different states of economic development – China and Japan

⊚ how and why China and Japan are geographically similar

⊚ how and why China and Japan are geographically different

⊚ why places such as China and Japan change

⊚ how countries such as China and Japan are linked together

⊚ how to locate places and environments.

E

F

G

H

**1** Before you begin finding out about another country, you need to think about what you already know or do not know about that country. You have learned about **perceptions** before – think carefully about country **stereotyping**.

**a** Make two lists, one for China and one for Japan. Write down in each list anything you already know about each country (e.g. main cities, industrial company names, sports personalities, people, events).

**b** Share your lists with a partner. How do they compare?

**c** Write down ten questions that you would like to ask to find out more about China and Japan.

**d** Can you think of any reasons why the Chinese name for China is 'the Middle Kingdom'?

**2** Look at photographs **C–H**.

**a** For the photographs that show people, decide what the people are doing (e.g. working, travelling, shopping, on holiday).

**b** For each photograph, study the landscape. What is it like? Classify them into types (e.g. flat, mountainous, countryside, built up, urban).

**c** Which photographs do you think were taken in China and which were taken in Japan? Write down where you think each one was taken and give a reason for your choice. (The actual locations of the photographs are given on page 92 – but don't cheat!)

**d** Write a suitable caption for each photograph.

# Where are China and Japan?

The first step of any geographical enquiry is to ask questions. Often the first question you need to ask is 'where are the places located?' You need maps, atlases and globes at a variety of different scales to answer this question fully.

Simply stating that China and Japan are both in the continent of Asia begins to locate these countries, but we can define them more accurately using lines of latitude and longitude.

Using map **A** we can see that China is between 20°N and 55°N (lines of latitude) and between 75°E and 135°E (lines of longitude).

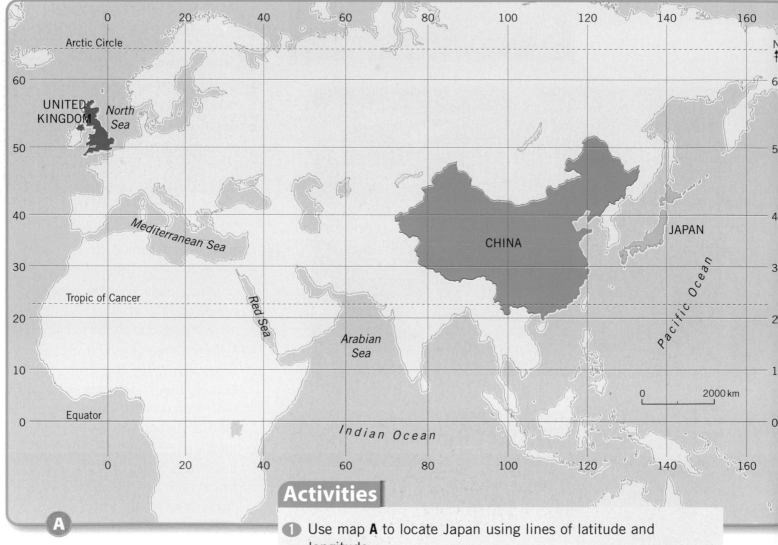

**A**

| Country | Land area (km²) |
|---------|-----------------|
| UK | 244 880 |
| China | 9 596 960 |
| Japan | 377 800 |

**B** How much land?

## Activities

1. Use map **A** to locate Japan using lines of latitude and longitude.

2. Estimate the central point of China and work out the latitude and longitude of this point. Do the same for Japan.

3. Look up China and Japan in the index of an atlas. What latitude and longitude reference is given for each country? Why do you think they give these references?

4. Work out the location of the UK using latitude and longitude.

| Country | Average population density (people per km$^2$) | Total population (millions of people) |
|---------|------------------------------------------------|---------------------------------------|
| UK      | 237                                            | 59                                    |
| China   | 126                                            | 1259                                  |
| Japan   | 332                                            | 126                                   |

**C** How many people?

**D** An image of Japan from a satellite – an island nation made from nearly 4000 different islands

**E** An image of the world, including China, from a satellite – China is a country large enough to be home to nearly a quarter of the world's population

## help!

✪ Remember that we are comparing these countries. How much bigger is China than Japan? How much larger is the population of China than that of Japan? Include this information in your summary paragraph.

## Activities

5 Study satellite images **D** and **E**. With the help of your atlas, make a list of the oceans and seas that surround the islands of Japan.

6 Make a list of the countries that have a border with China.

7 Write a short paragraph to summarise your answer to the question '*Where are China and Japan?*'

# China – where do people live and work?

The second step in a geographical enquiry is to decide what data is needed to answer the questions set out in Step one.

In 1999 the Chinese government estimated the population of China to be 1259 million, nearly one quarter of the world's population. The number of people affects every aspect of daily life, from family size, providing homes and jobs, to using resources. The population continues to increase (diagram **A**), even though the rate of increase has slowed down.

China's population is not evenly distributed throughout the country. In 2001 70 per cent of the people live in rural areas, while 30 per cent live in urban areas. However, this is changing and by 2025 the urban population is expected to be bigger than the rural population.

| | |
|---|---|
| **1 056 666** | a month |
| **243 846** | a week |
| **34 835** | a day |
| **1 451** | an hour |
| **24** | a minute |

**A** The increase in the Chinese population, 1996

**B** Urbanisation – a high density of people

**Key**
Population density
National average per sq km: 126
- Eastern region 383
- Central region 147
- Western region 51

N
0    120 km

**C** China's population density

D Rural areas – a low density of people

When the People's Republic of China was established in 1949, there was virtually no agricultural or industrial development. People's average life expectancy was just 32 years. Now China has one of the fastest-growing global economies: in 1990 it was the fifteenth largest trading nation in the world; by 1994 it was eleventh and by 1997, including Hong Kong, it was the fourth largest trading nation in the world. There are still differences between rural and urban living standards, but the average life expectancy is now 70 years.

F A wide range of products are made in China

E The changing nature of work, 1952–1996

Key
- Agriculture
- Manufacturing
- Services

| Year | Agriculture | Manufacturing | Services |
|------|-------------|---------------|----------|
| 1952 | 83.5% | 7.4% | 9.1% |
| 1965 | 81.5% | 8.3% | 10.2% |
| 1978 | 70.5% | 17.4% | 12.1% |
| 1986 | 60.9% | 21.9% | 17.2% |
| 1991 | 59.8% | 21.4% | 18.8% |
| 1996 | 50.5% | 23.5% | 26% |

# Activities

1 Study map **C**.

a Some parts of China have very few people. Write down the names of these areas.

b Some parts of China have very many people. List the names of these areas.

c Use an atlas to find where the main towns and cities are located. By 2025 it is expected that more people will live in cities than in rural areas. What do you think this will mean for the distribution of population?

2 Study graph **E**.

a Describe what has happened to the number of people who work in agriculture.

b Describe what has happened to the number of people who work in manufacturing and services.

c Where in China do you think it would be easier for people to find jobs – the east or the west? Explain why you think so.

d What difference will increased urbanisation make to the sorts of jobs that are available?

3 Write a short paragraph to summarise what you have found out about:

a Changes in where people live.

b Changes in jobs.

## Case Study
## What do we learn about China from the media?

**A** China Town in Liverpool

## What is the media?

The **media** is any method of communication which reaches large numbers of people. Sometimes stories in the media are not the whole story. The story or image of a place or country often just reflects what the person writing the newspaper article, or making the TV programme, thinks about the country. How does China come across in the media? If you only knew about China from information in the media, what sort of place would you think it is?

## Fact file

**Technical achievements in ceramics**

Chinese potters were making china that was fired to high temperatures of over 1200 °C nearly 3500 years ago – the Shang dynasty. It took more than 3000 years before countries in the western world developed the technical expertise to make similar china. High-fired, high-quality pottery is still called china. It is usually made from a type of very pure white clay called porcelain.

**B** China from China – a Tang dynasty pottery horse

## US to warn Beijing over stalled trade talks

*The Times, 12 October 2000*

## In the jaws of the Dragon

*The Guardian, 3 April 2001*

## China to build world's tallest dam

*The Guardian, 15 May 2001*

## UK exporters fear Chinese uncertainty

*The Times, 5 April 2001*

## China's dustbowl nightmare

*The Guardian, 13 June 2001*

## China puts US in check

*The Guardian, 5 April 2001*

## China puts gloss on labour camps to pacify West

*The Daily Telegraph, 20 May 2001*

## China anger at British attacks on human rights

*The Daily Telegraph, 1 December 2000*

**C** What the papers say

| | |
|---|---|
| 1 Renminbi | = 100 Yuan |
| 12 Renminbi | = £1 |

**D** Chinese currency

# Activities

1. Study photograph **A**. Make a list of the things that make this place distinctive as China Town. Who are these things for – the local people or tourists?

2. Read the fact file. Does China's long history of technical expertise match the image of China in the newspaper headlines (**C**)?

3. Study the newspaper headlines in **C**. Annotate each headline to show how China is portrayed. An example is given below.

### In the jaws of the Dragon

Why Dragon? The Chinese five-toed dragon is a symbol of happiness and good fortune. The Dragon stands for a wild, untamed, fierce creature in western cultures. The headline reflects an image of China as powerful (the jaws), mysterious and uncontrollable. In the West the headline is a threatening one. In China it would be difficult to understand. What does this say about the West's image of China? Why is it described in this way? Is China really like that?

4. The newspaper headlines in **C** will soon become out of date. Carry out your own newspaper search for headlines about China over a period of two or three weeks. Make a display of the headlines and annotate each one to explain how China is portrayed in each one. Your school library may have resources to help you.

5. Work in a small group to expand your media search. Monitor radio and TV news and compare the results.

6. Carry out an Internet search to find news articles on China. You could try the websites for:

   ⊚ BBC News
   ⊚ CNN News
   ⊚ Electronic Telegraph
   ⊚ Guardian Unlimited
   ⊚ Yahoo News

   at www.heinemann.co.uk/hotlinks

# China – the physical environment

B The Tibet plateau

C The Huang He River

D The Sichuan Basin

**Map A labels:** RUSSIA, KAZAKHSTAN, MONGOLIA, JAPAN, NORTH KOREA, SOUTH KOREA, Tarim Basin, Loess Plateau, Huang He River, CHINA, Sichuan Basin, Yangtze River, Plateau of Tibet, Yunnan–Guizhou Plateau, INDIA, TAIWAN, Pacific Ocean, South China Sea, PHILIPPINES, Indian Ocean, 0 500 km, N

A

Although China is large – some 9.5 million km² – it is possible to divide it into a number of distinctive landscapes (map **A**). The eastern part of the country is an area of river basins and plains, while the western part is either high mountains or high **plateau**. The high mountainous plateau of Tibet has an average height of 4000 metres. In the central plateau the Tarim Basin, the Loess Plateau, the Sichuan Basin and the Yunnan–Guizhou Plateau are all around 900 metres. The eastern river basin plains are around 700 metres.

The two largest rivers in China, the Huang He (Yellow River) and the Yangtze, flow from west to east.

Because China is so large the physical environment varies greatly. Environmental concerns include soil erosion and the effects of climate, from snow storms to droughts, and pollution from developing factories.

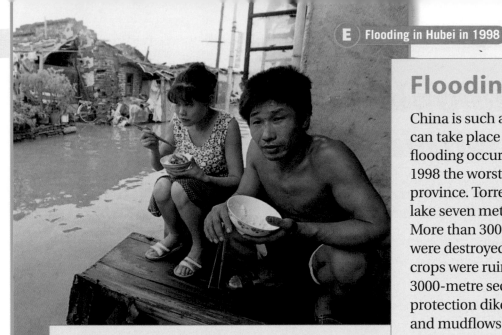

## Flooding

China is such a large country that localised flooding can take place in all parts of the country, but each year flooding occurs on the Yangtze and Huang He rivers. In 1998 the worst flooding for 44 years occurred in Hubei province. Torrential rains in July and August created a lake seven metres deep and covering nearly 325 km$^2$. More than 3000 people were killed, 2.9 million houses were destroyed and more than 9 million hectares of crops were ruined. Flood waters washed away a 3000-metre section of a newly constructed flood protection dike. Officials said that floods, landslides and mudflows affected some 240 million people – one fifth of China's population.

## Fire

Forest fires during the hot dry season can cause widespread damage. A total of 3021 people were killed and 4404 others injured in fires in China in 2000. Financial losses were more than 1.5 billion Yuan. The official Xinhua news agency said that tree felling as well as soil erosion following forest fires may have contributed to the flooding. Without the forest cover, rain flows quickly into the rivers, carrying large amounts of soil which silt up the river channels and cause flooding.

**F** Earthquake damage at Zhangjiapo village, China

## Earthquakes

China sits between two of the largest tectonic plate boundaries – the Pacific plate boundary lies to the east and the circum–Indian plate boundary lies to the south west. Since 1900 there have been more than 800 earthquakes of a magnitude of 6.0 or greater on the Richter scale.

China has had some success with predicting earthquakes. Even so, since 1900 nearly half a million people have died in earthquakes – 53 per cent of all the world's earthquake casualties.

On 10 January 1998 an earthquake of 6.2 on the Richter scale caused damage to more than nineteen cities and affected nearly 170 000 people in Zhangbei, Shangyi, Wanquan and Kangding. Forty-nine people were killed and 11 439 people were injured. The economic loss was put at 794 million Yuan.

### Activity

1 Copy and complete the hazard grid below. The first row has been done for you – add flooding, fire and earthquakes. You may want to leave some boxes blank.

| Hazard | Natural causes | Human causes | Effects | Location or details of damage |
|---|---|---|---|---|
| Soil erosion | Heavy rain and steep slopes | Deforestation | Soil washed away | Widespread in China |

# Are there regional differences within China?

It is clear that China has some parts of the country that are different from other parts of the country. But can you clearly identify these regions?

**Western China**
High mountains.
Colder at higher altitudes.
Very cold winters (below -10°C).
Lower air pressure.
Low rainfall (less than 500 mm a year).
Growing season of 6 months or less.

**Northern China**
Continental effects of being a long way from the sea.
Cold, dry air sinks.
Moderate rainfall.
Large temperature range.
Winds blowing from the north bring cold air.
Growing season of less than 6 months.

**Eastern seaboard**
Wetter air blowing from the sea picks up more moisture.
High rainfall (over 1000 mm a year).
Colder winters (below 10°C).
Growing season of 6–8 months.

**Southern China**
Hotter temperatures (up to 35°C).
Warm winters (above 10°C).
Limited temperature range.
High rainfall (over 1000 mm a year) because warm air can hold more moisture.
Growing season of more than 8 months.

N

0      500 km

**Key**
Height above sea level
Below 500 metres
500–2000 metres
Above 2000 metres

**A** China's climatic regions

## What do we mean by a region?

Geographers often try to classify different parts of countries into regions. The idea is to identify the features that make each area different. Of course, the real world does not always fit this idea of clear regions easily. For example, some features like climate or relief are easy to measure. Others, such as language differences, or political and economic characteristics, can be more difficult to identify. It is often difficult to know where one region ends and another begins – how do you draw lines in real places?

## Activities

1. Map **A** shows detailed information on climate for four regions of China. Copy and complete the table below to summarise the climate in each region. Add figures if you can!

|  | Rainfall | Temperature | Growing season |
|---|---|---|---|
| Western China |  |  |  |
| Southern China |  |  |  |
| Eastern seaboard |  |  |  |
| Northern China |  |  |  |

2. For each of the regions, work out the height of the land above sea level. How do you think this affects the climate?

**B** The United Nations Human Development Index (HDI) is based upon life expectancy, educational levels and income. This map shows the Chinese provinces ranked according to this index, where 1 is the best and 30 the worst

Key
1–5
6–10
11–15
16–20
21–25
26–30

## Activities

**3 a** Study map **B** and work out which provinces have the best HDI.

**b** Now look back at map **C** on page 74 showing population density. Are the provinces with the best HDI those that have low population densities or high population densities?

**4 a** On a base map of China, shade the three physical regions (lowlands, plateau and mountains).

**b** Make a series of three or four overlay maps. The first should show the areas of high population density and the major cities. What could you decide to show on the other overlays – climate, economic development, political provinces, HDI?

**c** Once you have completed your map and overlays, try to identify any different regions within China.

**5** Imagine you have been asked to give a five-minute talk to your local regional twinning organisation. Choose one of the regions you have investigated and write the script for your talk. Make sure you compare this region and your own.

**6 Extension**

**a** What sort of information do you need to compare regions?

**b** How does this differ from the information you need to compare countries?

### One country – two systems

In 1997 Hong Kong Island and the surrounding islands were returned to China as a Special Administrative Region (SAR). Some 6.2 million people live in the Hong Kong SAR. In the 1980s and 1990s Hong Kong developed a **democratic** system of government, which was one of the reasons why it has become a major economic centre. China still has a **centralised Communist** system of government. China calls this 'one country – two systems'.

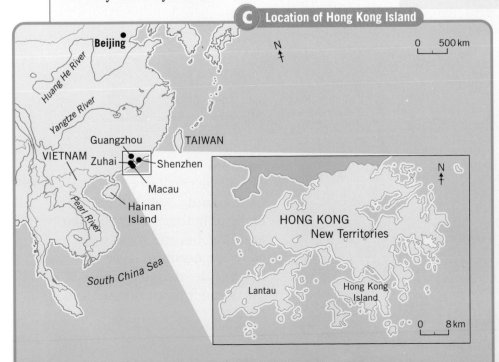

**C** Location of Hong Kong Island

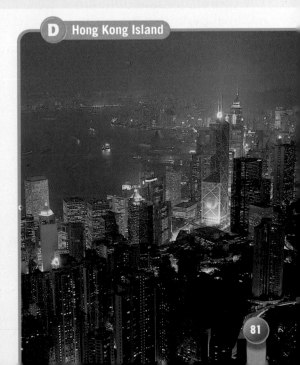

**D** Hong Kong Island

# Are there regional differences within Japan?

Just as Britain is divided into counties for local government, Japan is divided into 47 prefectures. These **prefectures** are then grouped into eight regions (map **A**).

## Tohoku

Honshu Island has five regions. Tohoku is the furthest in the north. It is Japan's main rice-growing region. It has recently been linked to other regions by a new expressway and bullet train. Sendai is becoming a centre for industry and offices.

## Hokkaido

The most northern island. Very few people live here. Jobs are mostly in farming and fishing, although tourism is becoming important.

## Chūbu

In the south along the Pacific coast it is mostly urban and industrial. The central mountainous areas are national parks that are easily accessible to many people. To the north, along the coast of the Sea of Japan, many nuclear power stations have been built.

Hokkaido

N

Tohoku

Chūbu

Kanto

Chugoku

Kinki

Shikoku

Kyushu

0    250 km

**A** Japan's prefectures and regions

## Kyushu

The north of the island, which has very good links to Honshu, is an old industrial area. Two-thirds of the population of the island live here. The south is mainly farming, but it is also popular with tourists who come for the sub-tropical climate and volcanic scenery.

## Shikoku

This is the smallest of the four main islands. New bridges are being built to connect Shikoku and Honshu, and these will allow the northern coast to become developed. The rest of the island is mountainous and remote.

**Kanto**

The largest concentration of population live in this region (see photo on page 71). Tokyo, the capital city, is a centre for manufacturing and service industries. The country's main port is at Yokohama. Kawasaki is one of the main areas for heavy industry. This region is sometimes called the 'heart' of Japan.

**Chugoku**

This region is remote and underdeveloped. The main city is Hiroshima. Inland it is mountainous.

**Kinki**

This is Japan's second most important industrial region. It contains three major cities: Kyoto, Osaka and Kobe.

# Activities

**1** Research photos of Shikoku and Kyushu from the internet or a CD-ROM encyclopedia. Print each photo and annotate them from the information on page 82.

**2** Use the photographs and information on these pages to list the physical and human features of the four islands of Hokkaido, Honshu, Shikoku and Kyushu. Copy the table below to help you to organise your ideas. Hokkaido has been started for you.

**3** Choose two photographs which you think show the contrasts between the different regions in Japan. Draw a sketch of each photograph and add annotations to show the contrasts in physical and human features.

**4** New road and rail links are planned to link Hokkaido with Honshu. How do you think this might change Hokkaido?

| Island | Physical features | Human features |
|--------|-------------------|----------------|
| Hokkaido | The photograph shows ... | Few people ... |
| Honshu | | |
| Shikoku | | |
| Kyushu | | |

# Japan – the physical environment

Most of Japan's islands are steep and mountainous so they are of little use for settlement. There are four main islands and about 3900 smaller ones. In fact, less than sixteen per cent of the country is classed as lowland. It is in this small area of lowland that settlement and economic activity must take place. Flat land is a scarce resource in Japan (map **A**).

The steep mountains that make up the 'backbone' of the four main islands are the result of movements between the tectonic plates. When the plates move, the result is often an earthquake or volcanic activity. Sometimes underwater earthquakes cause huge waves called *tsunami*.

**Key**
- ☐ Lowlands
- ☐ Foothills
- ☐ Mountains and uplands
- ▲ Main active volcanoes
- ▬ Volcanic zones
- ● Most violent earthquakes
- --- Plate boundary

N

0        250 km

**A** Japan's physical environment

## Activities

**1** The physical environment of Japan has provided both opportunities and difficulties for the Japanese people. Copy and complete the table below to balance each of the opportunities with the difficulties people face.

**2 a** Draw up a hazard grid for Japan like the one on page 79. Use the information on page 85 to complete it.

**b** What differences do you notice between hazards in China and Japan?

| Opportunities | Difficulties |
|---|---|
| Timber resources from the wooded mountains | |
| Hot springs in the volcanic areas | |
| Wilderness areas with spectacular scenery to encourage tourists | |
| A good climate for growing crops | |
| Fishing in the coastal waters around the islands | |

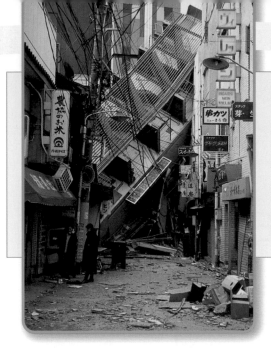

## Earthquakes

Kobe (left) is the sixth largest city in Japan. On 17 January 1995 it was shaken by a series of earthquakes. The largest reached 7.2 on the Richter scale. It was Japan's worst earthquake for almost 75 years. Nearly 6000 people were killed, some 26 000 were injured and up to 310 000 were left homeless. Some 75 000 buildings were damaged or destroyed. The repair bill was estimated at £60 billion.

## Volcanoes

In September 2000 Mount Oyama erupted again, forcing residents to flee. Smoke rose as high as 3000 metres. Experts said it was the highest level of activity recently observed from the 813-metre high volcano. About 630 people were ordered to evacuate the Tsubota and Kamitsuki areas. Here, a man tries to clean ash off his car.

## Floods and landslides

In 1997 heavy rains triggered 200 mudslides. The village of Izumi was hardest hit. Here, 80 families lived in a valley known to be vulnerable to landslides. The government recognised the threat and started to build a 16-metre high concrete barrier. But it proved to be no protection. At 1 am on 16 July an avalanche of bright red mud, boulders and trees roared down the hill, crashing right through the barrier.

## Typhoons

Typhoons (left) develop in warm tropical waters and have winds of at least 65 kph. An average of 28 typhoons form between June and September each year, but usually only two or three pass across Japan. There have been few disasters recently because of improved forecasting techniques and better methods of warning people. The worst recent typhoon killed 19 people in September 1991.

# Case Study

## What do we learn about Japan from the media?

| Word | | How to draw/write | Kanji |
|---|---|---|---|
| Paddy field |  | 丿冂冊用田 | 田 |
| Tree | | 二十才木 | 木　木木 (Woods)　森 (Forest) |
| Mountain | | 卜山山 | 山 |
| River | | 丿川川 | 川 |

**A** Japanese kanji

A major difference between Japan, China and western countries is the style of writing. Japanese writing developed from the Chinese system and in both systems the symbols represent something. The symbolic parts of the writing are called **kanji**. Diagram **A** shows how some of these symbols have come about, and how to draw them. It is important to follow the arrows as these have been developed to ensure legible handwriting!

**B** Map of Japan with labels in 'kanji'

# Menu

Traditional

Modern

**C** Breakfast menu – which would you choose?

'Rice' and 'food' mean almost the same thing in Japan. Breakfast is literally translated as 'morning rice', while lunch would be 'noon rice' and dinner 'evening rice'. But like many other aspects of Japanese life, attitudes are changing. Few young people would choose the traditional breakfast menu from diagram **C** nowadays.

**D** Traditional Japanese art

Japan was cut off from the rest of the world until the mid-nineteenth century. When contact was at last made, the people of Europe and America often treated the Japanese people as oriental curiosities and within a very short space of time the Japanese were described as 'naïve children' and 'inscrutable'.

Japanese art and culture, as well as the unfamiliar religious philosophies such as Shintō and Buddhism, seemed strange and mysterious. The overall western attitude was often prejudiced and based upon stereotypes. In recent years Japan has become very good at turning these negative images into positive ones. Many business managers around the world have studied Japanese management techniques. Zen meditation and Buddhism have many converts. The Japanese language is taught in an increasing number of UK schools.

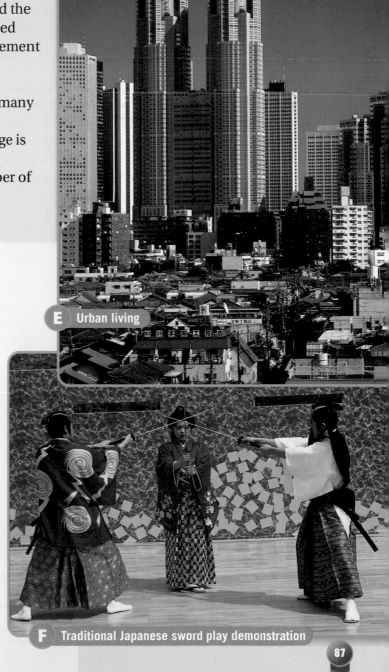

**E** Urban living

**F** Traditional Japanese sword play demonstration

# Activities

**1** **a** Make a sketch map of a small, imaginary Japanese island. Label it using some of the kanji symbols in diagram **A**.

**b** How easy did you find it to write the kanji? Why do you think this is?

**2** Study photographs **D**, **E** and **F**. Stereotypes are bad because they are based on biased and incomplete information.

**a** List the ways in which the information in the photographs is incomplete.

**b** What photographs would you take to balance these pictures to make the image complete? Look through the pictures of Japan in this unit to help you with ideas.

**3** **Extension**

How would you set about challenging stereotypes about Japan? (Pages 90 and 91 may give you some ideas.)

# Trading places?

On 19 May 2000 China joined the World Trade Organisation (photograph **A**). The central issue that had to be resolved before China could join the WTO was how European companies would be allowed access to the mobile phone market in China.

Trade is vital to both China and Japan's economic success. China's success as one of the world's largest trading nations is all the more remarkable because it has achieved this since 1978 when the **'open policy'** was declared. By 1997 China and Japan were each other's largest trading partner (diagram **B**), and both countries have economic links with the rest of the world.

But while China's economy has gone from strength to strength, Japan has suffered a 'slow down' in economic growth in the past ten years. In April 2000 the value of Japanese industries was lower than it had been in 1985. Consumers are spending less money, so to maintain any economic growth Japan has to trade with other countries. The result has been an increase in trade, investment and aid with China.

**A** China joins the World Trade Organisation

Japan and China are each other's largest trading partner

Japan 60.8

Hong Kong 50.8

Australia 5.3

Netherlands 5.5

France 5.6

UK 5.8

USA 49

Russia 6.1

South Korea 24

Singapore 8.8

Taiwan 19.8

Germany 12.7

In 1997, China's top twelve trading partners accounted for 78 per cent of China's total trade

*Figures in billions of US$*

**B** China's top twelve trading partners

## Getting Technical ▾

- **Exports** are goods or services that are sent out or sold to another country.

- **Invisible exports** are payments for services, for example transport, shipping, banking and tourism.

- **Visible exports** include items such as foodstuffs, raw materials and manufactured goods.

- **Imports** are goods and services that are brought in from another country through trade.

- **Balance of trade** is the difference in value between exports and imports. When a country exports more goods and services than it imports, it has a **trade surplus**.

**C** The top nine traders of the world

1613 European Union

1588 USA

760 Japan

415 Canada

402 Hong Kong (China)

★ 325 China

281 South Korea

235 Taiwan

224 Mexico

*Figures in billions of US$*

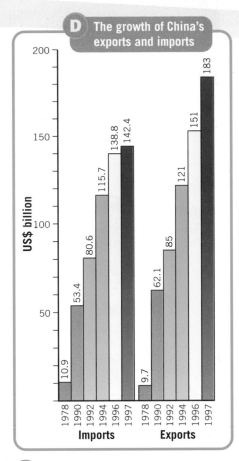

**D** The growth of China's exports and imports

US$ billion

Imports: 10.9, 53.4, 80.6, 115.7, 138.8, 142.4

Exports: 9.7, 62.1, 85, 121, 151, 183

Years: 1978, 1990, 1992, 1994, 1996, 1997

**Imports**     **Exports**

## Activities

1 Study graph **D**.
   a Work out the balance of trade between China and the rest of the world for each year.
   b Write a sentence to describe what changes in trade the graph shows. The text on page 88 will help you explain what the graph tells you about China's economy.

2 Since when has China had a trade surplus? What do you think China should spend this surplus on?

3 Study the information about Hong Kong here and on page 81. Write a short summary (no more than 30 words) to explain why Hong Kong is an important trading centre.

**E** Hong Kong

# Hong Kong, a special administrative region

Hong Kong grew originally because it was on a trade route and had a large, deep, sheltered harbour. It became part of China in 1997. The city is one of the world's most prosperous economies, and the population is growing rapidly. It is estimated that the number of people will increase from 6.7 million in 1999 to 8.2 million by 2015. Hong Kong is in the right place geographically and it is one of the main ports to import goods into mainland China. A new airport was recently built on Lantau island, which is linked to the mainland by road and rail bridges. A map to show the location of Hong Kong can be found on page 81.

# What links do China and Japan have with the UK?

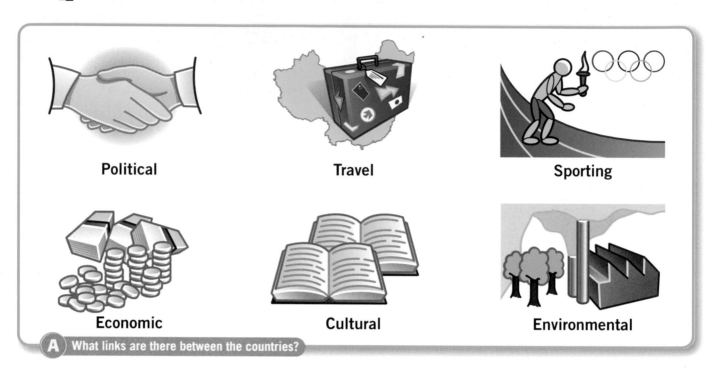

Political

Travel

Sporting

Economic

Cultural

Environmental

**A** What links are there between the countries?

Imports to the UK from China in 2000 £5 005 million

Exports to China from the UK in 2000 £1 468 million

Japan has a long history of economic links with the UK. The UK is Japan's main trading partner in Europe, and many Japanese companies have invested in factories in the UK (diagram **B** and photograph **C**). Between 1997 and 2001 the Japanese economy grew very little. However, the Chinese economy continues to thrive and in March 2001 it was growing at a rate of 8 per cent. Chinese exports were up by 28 per cent in 2000 and Chinese imports rose by 35 per cent.

**C** Japanese investment in high-tech factories in the UK (Mitsubishi, Scotland)

Imports to the UK from Japan in 1999 £9 251 million

Exports to Japan from the UK in 1999 £3 303 million

**B** Trade links between China, Japan and the UK

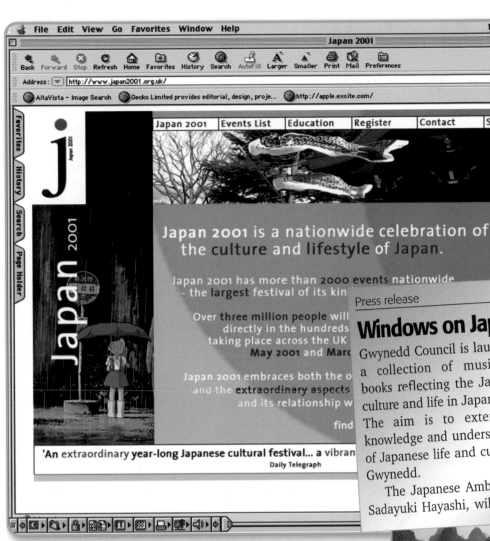

Japan 2001 is a nationwide celebration of the culture and lifestyle of Japan. Over two million people will participate in the hundreds of events taking place across the UK between May 2001 and March 2002. Japan 2001 celebrates both the ordinary and the extraordinary aspects of Japan and its relationship with the UK.

Press release

5 June 2001

## Windows on Japan

Gwynedd Council is launching a collection of music and books reflecting the Japanese culture and life in Japan today. The aim is to extend the knowledge and understanding of Japanese life and culture in Gwynedd.

The Japanese Ambassador, Sadayuki Hayashi, will launch the collection at Bangor Library on Saturday 9 June. The collection will tour Gwynedd's main libraries during the year.

Gwynedd Council has been working with the staff of the Institute of Japanese Studies, University of Wales, Bangor on this venture.

**D** Cultural links between Japan and the UK

**E** Travel links between China and the UK

## Activities

**1** Study box **D**, which shows some of the cultural links between the UK and Japan.

**a** What are cultural links?

**b** Why do you think Gwynedd Council in North Wales has set up the collection of books and music?

**c** What do you think the Japan 2001 series of cultural events hope to achieve? Why are events such as these important?

**d i** Choose one other type of link shown in diagram **A** and make a list of the activities and events that could be organised to strengthen this link.

  **ii** How would Japan and the UK benefit from these activities?

**2** Study diagram **B**.

**a** Work out the balance of trade between the UK and China and the UK and Japan.

**b** If the economy of Japan is not growing and the economy of China is growing, what would your economic forecast be for the way in which imports and exports from the UK to these countries will change?

**c** Do you think Chinese factories similar to the Japanese one in photograph **C** will be built in the UK? Explain your answer.

# Review and reflect

## Activities

**1** Look back at the list of ten questions you wrote down for question **1c** on page 71.

  **a** Have you found answers to them all?

  **b** Now you know more about Japan and China, would you like to change any of your questions? If so, which questions would you ask instead?

  **c** What sort of information was the hardest to find?

**2** Look back at the photographs on pages 70–71. The captions to the photographs are listed here. How do they compare with the captions you wrote?

**C** Great Wall of China

**D** Beijing centre

**E** Farmer in Nagano-ken, Japan

**F** Main road in Tokyo

**G** Japan NKK steelworks

**H** Volkswagen car plant, Shanghai, China

**3** Now you have collected your information, you can start to plan your report to compare Japan and China. Diagram **A** reminds you about the steps you need to take when carrying out a geographical enquiry.

You need to present your findings in the form of a report. There are many ways of doing this, not all of them written. Diagram **B** shows some ideas.

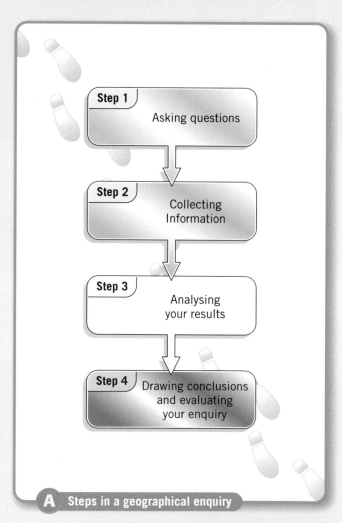

**Step 1** Asking questions

**Step 2** Collecting Information

**Step 3** Analysing your results

**Step 4** Drawing conclusions and evaluating your enquiry

**A** Steps in a geographical enquiry

**B** Reporting back

**Written report**

**Spoken report**

**Microsoft PowerPoint presentation**

**Published on a website**

**Wall display**

**Radio documentary**

**Series of posters**

# How to ...

**If you decide to present a written report, you might like to follow this structure:**

- *Introduction to set the scene* – What have you studied? What questions did you ask? Explain the focus of your report. Where are China and Japan? Define the terms you will use, e.g. economic development.

- *Data collection* – What data have you collected? How and where did you collect the data? How reliable is the data?

- *Analysis and explanation* – This is the most important section. Use as many ways to illustrate your data as possible, e.g. maps, diagrams, photographs, graphs, tables, charts and written paragraphs. Make sure you answer the questions you outlined in your introduction.

- *Conclusion and evaluation* – Look back at the focus of your report, which was to compare two countries at different stages of economic development. Use the things you have learned about as guidance, and write a summary paragraph for each one in your conclusion. Remember to evaluate what you have done, e.g. which parts of your enquiry went well, and which parts could have been improved.

- *List of sources (bibliography)* – Include a list of all the sources of data you used. Set them out like this:

  Book, article or website author; title; publisher; date of publication.

# 6 Virtual volcanoes and earthquakes

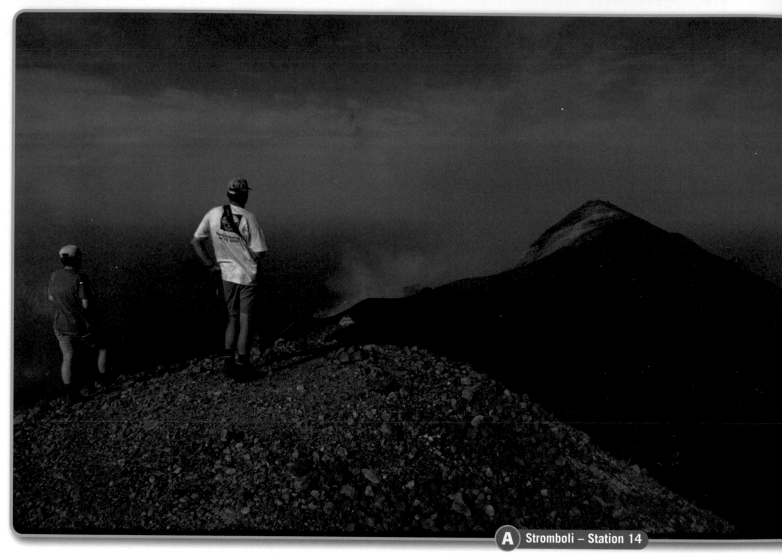

**A** Stromboli – Station 14

## Learn about

In this unit you are going to learn about

⊚ tectonic patterns and processes

⊚ the impact of these processes on countries that are at different stages of economic development

⊚ how to use the Internet to carry out enquiries about volcanoes and earthquakes.

**B** Aerial photo of Stromboli

# A virtual field trip up Stromboli

Stromboli is one of the Aeolian Islands, a group of volcanic islands located between Sicily and the Italian mainland, and it is one of the most active volcanoes on Earth. It has been in nearly continuous eruption for around 2000 years. The island is about 2 km in diameter. Its highest point is 924 metres above sea level but it rises over 3000 metres above the floor of the Tyrrhenian Sea.

In 1991 the population of the island was 361. However, during the summer months there are many more residents, mainly due to tourism.

**C** Location of Stromboli

## Activities

Imagine that your class is going on a one-day geography field trip to study Stromboli, an active volcano. Carry out some research using the website: 'Stromboli Online' at www.heinemann.co uk/hotlinks.

**1 a** Collect information using these headings:

- Population and settlement
- Transport
- Shops
- Weather and climate
- Vegetation
- Tourist information
- Health and safety (including possible hazards).

**b** When do you think is the best time of year to carry out the field trip?

**c** What else do you need to know in order to plan, and why?

**2** Choose the items you should carry up the volcano in your rucksack. To carry it comfortably, your backpack should weigh no more than 7.5 kg. Table **D** lists the possible items to choose from and their weights. To help you make sensible choices, use your research from question 1.

**3** Carry out a *virtual field trip* at 'Stromboli Online'.

**a** Before you begin, check out today's weather conditions using links from the website to both satellite images and weather stations (Napoli is the nearest).

**b** Choose whichever virtual route you prefer. As you ascend the volcano, collect the following information:

- the altitude at each station
- photographs
- at least one annotated field sketch
- changing vegetation types.

**4** At the end of the field trip evaluate your rucksack contents. Which were the good and poor choices? Why?

| Contents | Weight | Contents | Weight |
|---|---|---|---|
| 2 litres bottled water | 2 kg | Suntan lotion | 200 g |
| Food for one day | 1.5 kg | Sandals | 200 g |
| Trainers | 800 g | Clipboard | 200 g |
| Binoculars | 800 g | Spare T-shirt | 200 g |
| Jumper | 700 g | Hat | 150 g |
| Fleece | 600 g | Insect repellent | 100 g |
| Roll mat | 500 g | Swimsuit / trunks | 100 g |
| First aid kit | 500 g | Map | 50 g |
| Rucksack | 500 g | Pencils | 50 g |
| Camera and film | 500 g | Money bag | 50 g |
| Flask of hot drink | 400 g | Compass | 50 g |
| Towel | 300 g | Sunglasses | 50 g |
| Waterproof | 300 g | Change of socks | 50 g |
| Thermals | 300 g | Change of underwear | 50 g |
| Trowel | 300 g | | |
| Shorts | 250 g | | |

**D** Items that you might need on your trip

# What are volcanoes? Are they all identical?

Deep within the Earth it is so hot that some rocks melt to become a thick flowing substance called **magma**. Volcanoes are openings in the Earth's surface through which magma and ash erupt onto the land. Magma that has erupted is called **lava**.

Some volcanic eruptions are explosive and others are not. It depends on how runny or sticky the magma is. If magma is thin and runny, gases can escape from it so that it flows easily out of the volcano. Lava flows rarely kill anyone, because they move slowly enough for people to get out of their way, but they can destroy buildings in their path.

If magma is viscous (thick), gases cannot escape easily. Pressure builds up until the gases escape violently and explode. In this type of eruption, the magma blasts into the air and breaks apart into pieces called *volcanic bombs*. Explosive volcanic eruptions can be dangerous and deadly. They cause fiery clouds which race down mountainsides, destroying everything in their path. When hot volcanic materials mix with water from streams, *lahars* (mudflows) form. These can bury entire settlements.

There are many different ways to *classify* volcanoes. One is based on the shape of the volcanic landform. The most common types are:

⑥ strato volcanoes (sometimes called *composite*)

⑥ shield volcanoes.

Volcanoes of a third, less common type, **caldera complexes**, are huge and potentially very explosive. They often do not even look like volcanoes because when they erupt they collapse in on themselves rather than building up into a cone. The last major caldera complex eruption was Taupo in 83 AD. Other examples include Yellowstone, Rabaul and Toba.

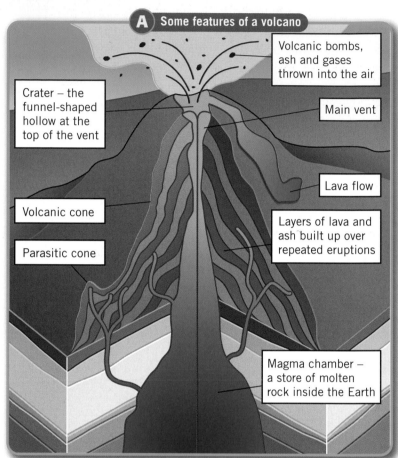

**A** Some features of a volcano

Volcanic bombs, ash and gases thrown into the air

Main vent

Lava flow

Layers of lava and ash built up over repeated eruptions

Magma chamber – a store of molten rock inside the Earth

Crater – the funnel-shaped hollow at the top of the vent

Volcanic cone

Parasitic cone

## Getting Technical ▼

### ⑥ Classification

It is often helpful to try to *classify* features such as volcanoes to make it easier to understand them. When you classify things you start to identify patterns, and these patterns may lead to a better understanding of whatever it is you are classifying. When you are classifying, you must remember that classification criteria are made up by humans – some volcanoes may not perfectly match the criteria. There will always be exceptions to your classification, and there will always be things that fall into more than one category.

# Strato volcanoes

Strato volcanoes make up 60 per cent of the Earth's volcanoes and are formed from layers of lava and ash. Their lava tends to be viscous (thick) and flows very slowly. This causes them to form steep-sided volcanic domes. The viscous lava also allows gas pressures to build up, causing explosive eruptions. Examples of strato volcanoes include Mount St Helens, Stromboli, Pinatubo, Mount Fuji, Merapi, Arenal and Cotopaxi.

**B** Arenal, Costa Rica

# Shield volcanoes

Shield volcanoes are the largest volcanoes on Earth. Shield volcanoes erupt lava that is very fluid. For this reason these volcanoes are not steep – the lava runs downhill too easily to form a pile. They also have very broad bases. Eruptions at shield volcanoes mainly consist of fountains of lava and lava flows. The Hawaiian shield volcanoes, Kilauea and Mauna Loa, are famous examples.

**C** Mauna Loa, Hawaii

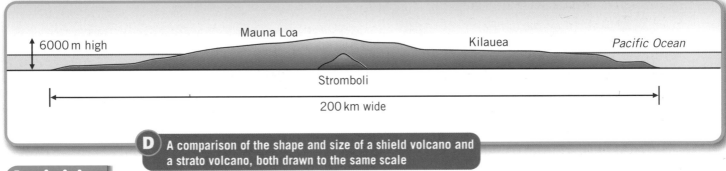

Mauna Loa

6000 m high

Kilauea

*Pacific Ocean*

Stromboli

200 km wide

**D** A comparison of the shape and size of a shield volcano and a strato volcano, both drawn to the same scale

## Activities

**1** Carry out an Internet enquiry into the characteristics of volcanoes across the world using the website 'Volcano World' at www.heinemann.co.uk/hotlinks. Draw a table in Word, like the one below, into which you can copy and paste your information. Add an extra column for satellite images and photographs if you wish. Begin with the volcanoes named on these two pages. **ICT**

| Name of volcano | Location | | Height | Type | Date of last eruption | Number of deaths | Features of eruptions |
|---|---|---|---|---|---|---|---|
| | Country | Continent | | | | | |
| Stromboli | Italy | Europe | 924 m | Strato | Continuous | 4 in 1919<br>4 in 1930<br>4 in 1986 | Small gas explosions with blobs of lava thrown up. Explosions each hour. |

**2** Create a word bank with definitions for the vocabulary you have included in your table.

**3** Plot the location of each of the volcanoes in your table onto a blank world map.

**4** In pairs, sort the table's contents according to the information in the different columns. Use this investigation to suggest at least one other system for classifying volcanoes. Be specific about the criteria you would use.

# What are earthquakes?
# Are they all identical?

## Case Study

All the case study information on pages 98 and 99 is from the *BBC Online* website. It is a small selection of their news reports following the devastating Gujarat earthquake which struck India in January 2001.

### Fact file: Gujarat, January 2001

- **Time and date:** 8.46 am local time on 26 January 2001.
- **Strength:** 7.9 on the Richter Scale – India's biggest earthquake since 1956. Tremors were felt as far away as Bangladesh.
- **Epicentre:** Near the town of Bhuj in Gujarat state, north-west India.
- **Level of Economic Development:** India is an **LEDC**.

Quake epicentre near Bhuj

**A** Area affected by the Gujarat earthquake, 2001

## What happened during the earthquake?

Dear Viki

I was just getting up and suddenly felt that a large group of monkeys were running around in the terrace because the room was shaking. The shakings didn't stop and became more severe. It was then that I suspected something big on the lines of an earthquake, but I couldn't believe it because Ahmadabad had never been hit by one.

I cannot describe the shaking to you. Just imagine how you would feel if someone very powerful took hold of your house and started shaking it right from the foundations. After about a minute it stopped. I have been lucky, by God's grace.

Vivek

**B** An e-mail from Vivek Iyer, an Ahmadabad doctor

## The effects on buildings and infrastructure

Many lives could have been saved in the Gujarat earthquake if building codes had been enforced and cheap protection measures carried out, Indian scientists say.

One civil engineer from Bombay said: 'We are beginning to learn that governments are not prepared. They directly or indirectly contribute to the deaths by permitting poor construction quality.'

India, along with other developing countries, is undergoing rapid urbanisation, so buildings are being put up quickly to meet growing housing needs. Some developers, keen to make a quick profit, are not as concerned about safety as they should be.

**C**

## • The effects on the people •

At least 30 000 people are estimated to have died in the quake. Another 55 000 have been injured and about half a million made homeless.

The authorities have turned their attention to long-term help for survivors, including setting up tent cities to shelter those made homeless by the quake.

As hopes of finding survivors fade, aid agencies are now trying to provide food, shelter and water to the families without homes.

Efforts are focusing on the need to cremate the thousands of dead to prevent the spread of disease. Many hospitals are treating people in the open air, and doctors say they are running out of bandages and medical supplies.

**D** News report, 30 January 2001

**F** Earthquake fault, Gujarat

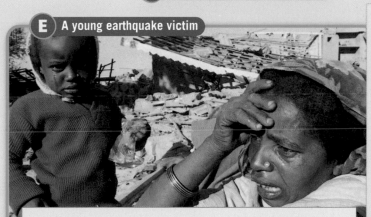

**E** A young earthquake victim

### Short-term responses to the earthquake

Aid from around the world has been pouring into India's earthquake zone. In a rare act, a plane from India's long-time rival Pakistan arrived carrying 2500 blankets and 200 tents for the quake survivors.

The United Nations Children's Fund has committed at least US $8 million in immediate aid. They have delivered thousands of blankets, a million chlorine tablets for purifying water, and plastic sheeting for shelter.

The UK, which has a large Indian community, has donated £10 million. It has also sent a team of 69 rescue workers on a military plane. Russia has sent a 59-strong team of medical and rescue experts, including doctors, a field hospital, and three dog teams.

**G** News report, 1 February 2001

## The effects on the economy

### The cost of India's quake

Gujarat is India's second largest industrial region, with many steel and textile mills. It has India's busiest port, Kandla. This earthquake will have an impact way beyond its state borders. Repairing buildings and installations is expected to cost around 150 billion rupees (£2.2 billion). It is an expense that India can ill afford. The government has asked the World Bank for a £1.1 billion loan to aid the rebuilding.

### Industries hit

The diamond, pharmaceuticals and textile industries are likely to be worst hit by the massive disruption to power lines, transport and telecommunications.

India's businesses are generally underinsured, so that more of the costs will be carried by local firms and individuals. Jobs will be lost and overall industrial production will fall. But steel and cement industries are likely to benefit from rebuilding the earthquake-hit region.

**H** News report, 2 February 2001

② Present your earthquake case study under the following headings:
- ⊚ What happened
- ⊚ Effects on buildings and infrastructure
- ⊚ Short- and long-term responses
- ⊚ Effects on the economy
- ⊚ Effects on the people

③ Add the geographical terms you have used to your word bank. 📖

④ Compare your earthquake case study with those of others in your class.

⑤ Plot the locations of each of the earthquake case studies onto the same world outline map as your volcanoes in the activities on page 97.

## Activities

You can find the BBC Online website at
www.heinemann.co.uk/hotlinks
Follow the links to *one* recent earthquake to produce a **case study** like this one. (ICT)

① Produce a fact file like the one on page 98 to introduce your earthquake case study.

# Where do earthquakes and volcanoes occur?

## Activities

Map **A** was taken from the earthquake area of the National Earthquake Information Centre website. Answer these questions using the map and an atlas.

**1** In which country was the most recent earthquake event?

**2** What was the strength and depth of this earthquake?

**3** What was the depth of the deepest recent earthquake? In which country did it happen

**4** What was the strength of the strongest earthquake? In which country did it happen?

**5** Did any of these earthquakes make the news in the UK? If so, why?

**6** Now download today's national earthquake map from the United States Geological Survey (see www.heinemann.co.uk/hotlinks). Use this map to answer questions **1–5** above.

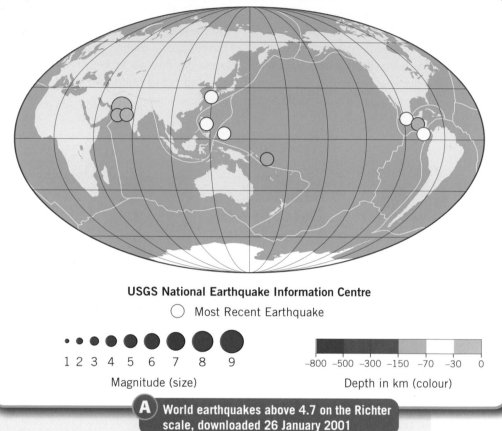

**USGS National Earthquake Information Centre**

○ Most Recent Earthquake

1 2 3 4 5 6 7 8 9
Magnitude (size)

–800 –500 –300 –150 –70 –30 0
Depth in km (colour)

**A** World earthquakes above 4.7 on the Richter scale, downloaded 26 January 2001

The Earth's crust is divided into about fifteen segments called **tectonic plates**. These plates 'float' on the mantle. Heat from within the Earth creates movements in the mantle. These cause the tectonic plates to move slowly, sometimes only a few centimetres per year.

Plates can move towards, away from or past one another. The boundaries where the plates meet are called **plate margins**. These are **active zones** because this is where most of the world's earthquakes and volcanic eruptions occur. There are two types of crust.

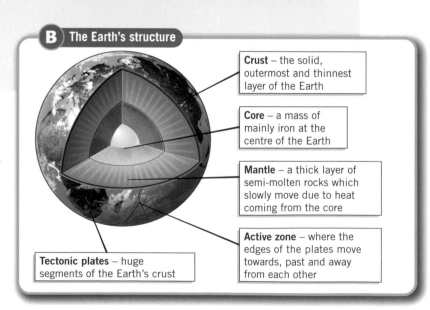

**B** The Earth's structure

**Crust** – the solid, outermost and thinnest layer of the Earth

**Core** – a mass of mainly iron at the centre of the Earth

**Mantle** – a thick layer of semi-molten rocks which slowly move due to heat coming from the core

**Active zone** – where the edges of the plates move towards, past and away from each other

**Tectonic plates** – huge segments of the Earth's crust

⊚ *Continental crust* is lighter, thick (35–70 km) and very old (over 1500 million years).

⊚ *Oceanic crust* is heavier, thin (6–10 km) and young (mostly less than 200 million years).

**C** Active zones found at tectonic plate margins

| Type of plate margin | Description of what happens | |
|---|---|---|
| **Constructive margin** | Two plates move away from each other and magma rises to the surface to form new crust. | |
| **Destructive margin** | Oceanic crust moves towards continental crust but, being heavier, it sinks beneath the continental rock and is destroyed. | |
| **Collision zone** | Plates made of continental crust move towards each other. They cannot sink so they crumple upwards to form **fold mountains**. | |
| **Conservative margin** | Two plates move past each other. Crust is neither formed nor destroyed. | |

## Activities

Compare your world map of earthquake and volcano locations from pages 97 and 100 with map **C** above.

1. On what types of plate margins do earthquakes tend to happen?

2. On what types of plate margins do volcanoes tend to erupt?

3. Use a world physical map in an atlas to name two fold mountain ranges at collision zones.

4. The Andes are also fold mountains.
   a On which type of plate margin are they located?
   b Name the two plates which are causing the Andes to form.

# What causes earthquakes and volcanoes?

## Active zones at destructive plate margins

Active zones at destructive margins occur where a plate made of oceanic crust moves towards a plate made of continental crust. The oceanic crust is heavier, so it is forced beneath the lighter continental crust and forms a **deep sea trench**. Because the plates do not slide smoothly past one another, there is often a huge build up of tension. If the crust breaks, shock waves are sent out in all directions. This is called an earthquake. The point where the crust breaks is called the **focus**. The place where the shock waves reach the Earth's surface is called the **epicentre**.

**A** Stromboli erupting

As the oceanic crust pushes beneath the continental crust, it melts. This is partly due to the heat caused by friction between the plates and partly due to the increase in temperature as it reaches the mantle. This creates magma which escapes to the surface along lines of weakness in the Earth's crust called **faults** to form volcanoes. Volcanic eruptions at destructive plate margins can be very violent.

## Case Study

### What caused Stromboli to form?

*Stromboli* has formed as a result of repeated volcanic eruptions which have built up layers of lava and ash to create a **strato volcano**. These eruptions are caused by the movement of the *African Plate* and the *Eurasian Plate* towards each other. As the *African Plate* is forced beneath the lighter *Eurasian Plate*, it heats up and melts. If the pressure on this magma builds up, it eventually rises to the Earth's surface to form volcanoes such as *Vesuvius*, *Etna* and *Stromboli*. The movement of these two plates towards one another also causes the crust to crumple upwards to form fold mountains such as the *Atlas Mountains* in *North Africa* and the *Apennines* in Italy.

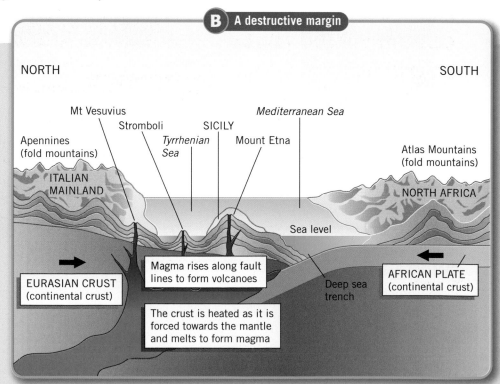

**B** A destructive margin

NORTH

SOUTH

Mt Vesuvius
Stromboli
SICILY
*Mediterranean Sea*
Apennines (fold mountains)
*Tyrrhenian Sea*
Mount Etna
Atlas Mountains (fold mountains)

ITALIAN MAINLAND

NORTH AFRICA

Sea level

Magma rises along fault lines to form volcanoes

EURASIAN CRUST (continental crust)

Deep sea trench

AFRICAN PLATE (continental crust)

The crust is heated as it is forced towards the mantle and melts to form magma

# Active zones at collision plate margins

An area where two plates made of continental crust move towards one another is called a **collision zone**. Because neither plate can sink beneath the other, their crust is crumpled upwards to form **fold mountains**, such as the Himalayas. These mountains are still increasing in height as the Indian Plate moves into the Eurasian Plate at a rate of about 5 cm per year, as measured using satellite images. Sometimes, as with destructive margins, tension may build up over time. Eventually the crust will break, sending out shock waves – an earthquake.

# Active zones at conservative plate margins

At conservative margins two plates move past one another, as in the case of the North American and Pacific Plates on the west coast of California (see **D**). Although the plates are travelling in the same direction, the Pacific Plate is moving faster, causing the plate margins to 'grind' past each other.

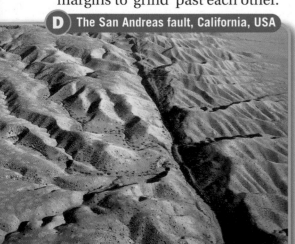

**D** The San Andreas fault, California, USA

## Case Study

### What caused the Gujarat earthquake, 26 January 2001?

The earthquake which hit *Gujarat State* in *north-east India* on *26 January 2001* was caused by the *Indian Plate* moving *north* towards the *Eurasian Plate* (see **C**). As both plates are made of continental crust, neither can sink so they crumple upwards. This causes tension to build up in the *Eurasian Plate*. This strain eventually made the crust break, causing an earthquake with a focus at a shallow depth of *16 km*. The epicentre was close to the town of *Bhuj*.

North          Himalayas (fold mountains)          South

KAZAKHSTAN                                          INDIA

INDIAN OCEAN

Bhuj

Focus of Gujarat earthquake, January 2001; 7.9 on Richter Scale and 10 km deep

EURASIAN PLATE (continental crust) almost stationary

INDIAN PLATE (continental crust) moving north

Mantle

Collision zone – crust crumples and faults

**C** A collision margin

As with destructive margins, when the two plates 'stick' it causes tension to build up. When this tension is suddenly released an earthquake occurs. Earthquakes happen daily along the San Andreas fault, but major events, causing loss of life, are much less frequent. The 1994 Los Angeles earthquake measured 6.6 on the Richter Scale and caused 60 deaths. At conservative margins, crust is neither created nor destroyed, so volcanic eruptions do not occur.

**E** A conservative margin

North American Plate moving north-westwards by 1 cm per year

San Andreas Fault

San Francisco

PACIFIC OCEAN

N

Los Angeles

Pacific Plate moving north-westwards by 6 cm per year

WEST

CANADA

NORTH AMERICA

New York

ATLANTIC OCEAN

Mid-Atlantic Ridge

Azores

Volcanic islands such as Iceland and the Azores

ICELAND

EUROPE

SPAIN

EAST

NORTH AMERICAN PLATE (oceanic crust) moving west

EURASIAN PLATE (oceanic crust) moving east

Magma from the mantle rises to form new crust

The North American Plate and the Eurasian Plate are moving apart at a rate of 5 cm per year

**F** **A constructive margin**

# Active zones at constructive plate margins

At constructive margins two plates move away from one another, as in the case of the North American and Eurasian Plates (see **F**). This type of movement happens mostly under oceans. As the plates move apart magma rises from the mantle to form new oceanic crust. This creates a line of underwater volcanoes along the plate margins called a **mid oceanic ridge**. In places the volcanoes become large enough to appear above sea level as volcanic islands such as Iceland. The type of volcano most often formed at a constructive plate margin is a shield volcano.

## Activities

**1 What causes a volcanic eruption?**

Choose one of the volcanoes you studied when you carried out your Internet Enquiry on page 97. Carry out the following activities based on that volcano.

**a** Name the type of plate margin on which the volcano is located using figure **C** on page 101.

**b** Draw a large annotated diagram (A4 size) to show how this volcano was formed. Use diagram **B** on page 102 or diagram **F** on this page for guidance.

⑥ Use an atlas to name actual places and features on your diagram, e.g. countries, plates, mountain ranges.

⑥ Make sure that you use the correct key words in your annotations.

⑥ Give your diagram a title – include in it the name of the volcano and the type of plate margin.

**c** The Case Study boxes on pages 102 and 103 demonstrate how to explain the causes of volcanic eruptions and earthquakes. Use these to help you to write a paragraph explaining how the volcano you have drawn was caused.

Make sure you:

⑥ use the correct key words – these appear in **bold print** in this unit

⑥ name actual places and features which are specific to the location of your volcano – these appear in *italics* in the Case Study boxes.

**2 What causes an earthquake?**

Carry out the following activities based on the earthquake in your case study (page 99).

**a** Name the type of plate margin on which the earthquake happened. Use figure **C** on page 101.

**b** Draw a large annotated diagram (A4 size) to show why this earthquake occurred. Use diagrams **B**, **C** and **E** on pages 102–104 and the bullet points in activity **1b** opposite for guidance.

**c** Write a paragraph explaining how the earthquake you have drawn was caused. Use the bullet points in activity **1c** for guidance.

# How do people live with earthquakes and volcanoes?

Earthquakes may be inevitable, but some earthquake disasters are not. Scientists and engineers work to understand earthquake hazards. This helps people to prepare for future earthquakes, especially in active zones which are very densely populated. They can try to predict the earthquake, and reduce the damage by being better prepared.

## How can earthquakes be predicted?

If scientists can predict when and where an earthquake will happen, people can be warned and lives saved, so scientists **monitor** active zones.

◉ Sensitive instruments measure earth movements and check the strain building up in rocks.

◉ The number of earthquakes can be plotted to show if a major earthquake is likely. Figure **A** shows that a major earthquake is expected around San Francisco Bay in the next thirty years.

◉ Several earthquakes often strike in a short time. **Foreshocks** occur before some large earthquakes, so scientists can work out the chances of a larger **mainshock** following. In August 1989 a shock of magnitude 5.1 struck near San Francisco. The public was warned that a larger quake could follow. Sixty-nine days later, 63 people were killed by the Loma Prieta quake, magnitude 7.1.

◉ **Hazard shaking maps** (see **B**) show the risk of earthquakes. They can help governments to plan emergency services and earthquake education. Engineers can plan earthquake codes for buildings, bridges and roads.

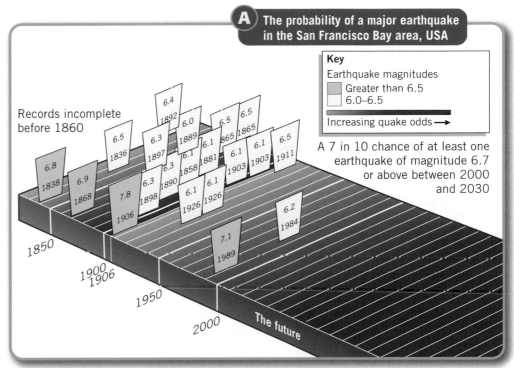

**A** The probability of a major earthquake in the San Francisco Bay area, USA

**Key**
Earthquake magnitudes
Greater than 6.5
6.0–6.5
Increasing quake odds →

A 7 in 10 chance of at least one earthquake of magnitude 6.7 or above between 2000 and 2030

Records incomplete before 1860

**Key**
Zone I: Very low damage risk
Zone II: Low damage risk
Zone III: Moderate damage risk
Zone IV: High damage risk
Zone V: Very high damage risk

**B** A hazard shaking map of India

# How can people prepare for earthquakes?

## Building codes

Many people are killed when earthquakes destroy buildings. Scientists can test how buildings respond to quakes, and improve their ability to survive, by using quake tables or platforms. The world's largest quake table is in Tsukuba Science City, Japan. It can carry buildings of up to 300 tonnes. Photo **C** shows a smaller shake table being used to test houses in India. Houses are built on a platform mounted on rollers, which is shaken by a tractor. The building on the right of the photo, made with cement mortar, collapses but the other, built with mud mortar, survives.

**C**  A low-cost shake table in Latur, India

## Education

People in Japan practise earthquake drills every year on 'Disaster Day' – 1 September. Similar drills are carried out in other places where earthquakes are a hazard, for example by practising DROP, COVER, AND HOLD ON (see the Red Cross website at www.heinemann.co.uk/hotlinks).

## Emergency services and relief

Governments must plan carefully to make sure the emergency services are prepared for possible earthquakes, and that relief supplies are ready. Good communication with earthquake monitoring stations can also save lives. This may be a problem for countries that cannot afford monitoring equipment and sophisticated communications.

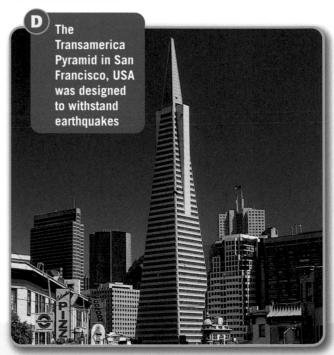

**D**  The Transamerica Pyramid in San Francisco, USA was designed to withstand earthquakes

## Activities  ICT

The information on pages 105 and 106 is about how people predict and prepare for earthquakes to try to reduce their effects. Carry out an Internet enquiry into how people predict and prepare for volcanic eruptions.

◎ Answer the questions using the websites and links available at www.heinemann.co.uk/hotlinks.

◎ Include case study information and illustrations.

### How can volcanic eruptions be predicted?

1 How can volcanoes be monitored?

2 What signs suggest a volcano may soon erupt?

### How can people prepare for volcanic eruptions?

3 How are eruption warnings given?

4 How can the public be better informed about volcanic hazards?

5 What should people do if a volcano erupts?

**help!**

○ Type the enquiry questions into a Word document.

○ Copy and paste relevant information from the websites under each question.

○ Highlight in red the most relevant information, then delete the rest.

○ Put the text into a logical order.

○ Insert side headings for each section of information.

# Review and reflect

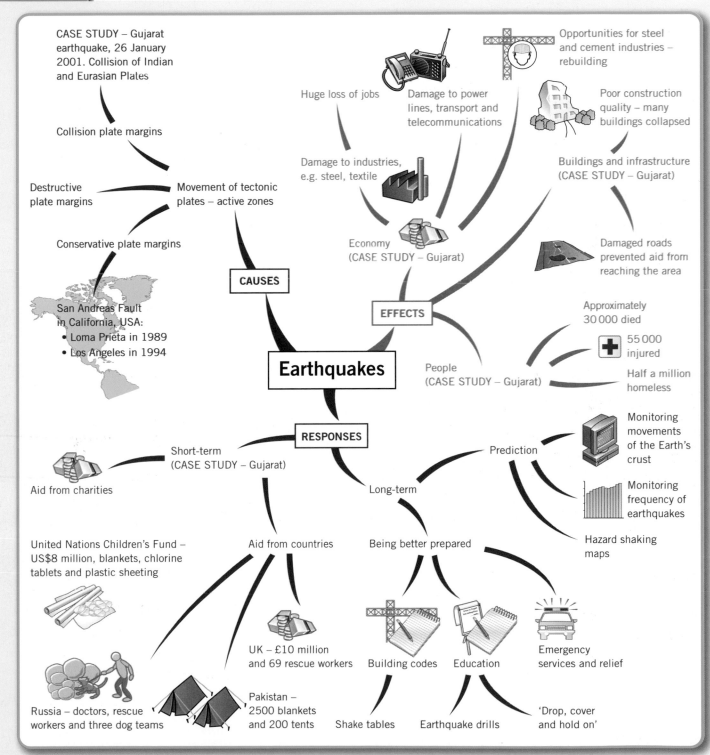

CASE STUDY – Gujarat earthquake, 26 January 2001. Collision of Indian and Eurasian Plates

Collision plate margins

Destructive plate margins

Movement of tectonic plates – active zones

Conservative plate margins

San Andreas Fault in California, USA:
- Loma Prieta in 1989
- Los Angeles in 1994

**CAUSES**

Huge loss of jobs

Damage to power lines, transport and telecommunications

Opportunities for steel and cement industries – rebuilding

Poor construction quality – many buildings collapsed

Damage to industries, e.g. steel, textile

Buildings and infrastructure (CASE STUDY – Gujarat)

Economy (CASE STUDY – Gujarat)

Damaged roads prevented aid from reaching the area

**EFFECTS**

Approximately 30 000 died

55 000 injured

People (CASE STUDY – Gujarat)

Half a million homeless

**Earthquakes**

**RESPONSES**

Short-term (CASE STUDY – Gujarat)

Aid from charities

Long-term

Prediction

Monitoring movements of the Earth's crust

Monitoring frequency of earthquakes

Hazard shaking maps

United Nations Children's Fund – US$8 million, blankets, chlorine tablets and plastic sheeting

Aid from countries

Being better prepared

Russia – doctors, rescue workers and three dog teams

UK – £10 million and 69 rescue workers

Pakistan – 2500 blankets and 200 tents

Building codes

Education

Emergency services and relief

Shake tables

Earthquake drills

'Drop, cover and hold on'

① The mind map above shows a summary of the earthquake information covered in this unit. Use it as a model to draw a similar mind map for the volcano information you have collected. You should begin with the heading VOLCANOES in the centre and the three sub-headings of CAUSES, EFFECTS and RESPONSES. Add the facts from your own research as well as including information from the textbook.

# 7 Cars on the Internet

## The global car industry

Making cars is one of the world's growth industries. In 2000, sales for passenger cars around the world rose to 49.4 million, the highest ever. The demand for all vehicles, including trucks and vans, increased to 58.2 million. As graph **A** shows, sales of new cars have grown steadily over the past twenty years. However, car sales and production are unevenly distributed around the world (table **B** and map **C**).

**A** World car sales, 1983–2000

Unit sales (millions)
1984 86 88 90 92 94 96 98 2000

Source: *The World's Car Manufacturers, Edition 4*

| Region | Number of new cars sold |
|--------|------------------------|
| USA, Canada and Mexico | 19 770 000 |
| South America | 1 922 000 |
| Western Europe | 15 120 000 |
| Eastern Europe | 2 592 000 |
| Middle East | 1 017 000 |
| Africa | 619 000 |
| Japan | 4 230 000 |
| Asia except Japan | 3 520 000 |
| Australia/New Zealand | 645 000 |
| **World** | **49 435 000** |

**B** New car sales, 2000

**C** Global car production

17 384 000 — USA, Canada and Mexico
15 397 000 — Western Europe
2 703 000 — Eastern Europe
4 803 000 — Asia except Japan
263 000 — Middle East
8 255 000 — Japan
1 665 000 — South America
228 000 — Africa

**D** Launch of the new Mini

**E** Demonstrations against the closure of the Longbridge plant in 2000

**F** Using technology to make cars

**Learn about**

In this unit you will learn about:

⊚ the global car industry

⊚ changes in the car industry in the UK

⊚ BMW, a global car producer

⊚ the car industry in Europe.

You will use the Internet to gain information on the car industry, to find out people's opinions on changes in the car industry, and as a way of communicating your findings and feelings to fellow pupils.

## Activities

**1** In pairs, discuss graph **A** and photographs **D–F**. What do they tell you about changes in the car industry? Share your ideas before making a list of the changes.

**2** Use the data in table **B** to draw located bars showing new car sales on a world map. You will need a base outline map of the world. ⓵②③

**3 a** Describe the pattern of global car production shown on map **C**.

**b** Compare car manufacturing (map **C**) with the map you have drawn to show car sales.

**c** Explain your findings. For example:

⊚ suggest reasons why some regions have high or low sales

⊚ suggest reasons why some regions make many or few cars.

## Research activity ⓘⓒⓣ

**4** Use the Internet to investigate the global car industry.

**a** As with any other sort of enquiry, good geographers start by asking questions. Work in pairs to think of the questions you might want to ask about the car industry. Use the Six Ws to help you: **W**hat? **W**here? **W**ho? **W**hen? **W**hy? Ho**W**? and aim to list two or more questions for each. For example:

⊚ Where are cars produced?

⊚ What changes are occurring?

**b** Visit the auto industry website through www.heinemann.co.uk/hotlinks. This site includes data on car production for the UK, Europe and the world. To find out about world car production, click on the World icon once you have opened the website.

**c** Choose one or two key pieces of information from the website which help to answer each of your questions. When you present them, remember to say what the information tells you.

**d** Which questions turned out to be difficult to answer from the website?

## How to ...

### ... draw located bar charts

**1** Map **C** shows you how to draw located bars.

**2** Use a similar scale for your map of car sales. Try a scale of 2 mm = 1 million new cars sold.

## help!

Good geographers look for key points when describing and explaining global patterns. Clever geographers make it sound easy! For example, consider:

⊛ which regions are the largest producers?

⊛ which regions are the less important producers?

⊛ are most of the producers MEDCs or LEDCs?

⊛ are they in the northern hemisphere (north of the Equator) or in the southern hemisphere (south of the Equator)?

⊛ are there any exceptions?

# The UK car industry

**A** BMW's factory at Cowley, Oxford

Most car **manufacturers** look for a number of **factors** when they are building a new factory. These include:

- a large area of cheap, flat land
- good **communications**
- a reliable and skilled workforce
- a nearby **market** for selling cars
- supporting industries that make **components**.

The UK's car industry is very important to the country's economy. About 790 000 jobs depend on it, including about 330 000 workers directly employed in making vehicles and components. The UK has over twenty motor vehicle manufacturers, but six **multinational companies** produce almost three-quarters of all cars. They are:

- Ford (including Jaguar and Land Rover)
- Vauxhall (owned by General Motors)
- Peugeot
- Honda
- Nissan
- Toyota.

**B** The location of Cowley

**C** The new Mini assembly line

## Changes in jobs

The car industry changes rapidly. Since the 1960s many UK car firms have been taken over by rival firms and some have gone out of business altogether. For example, in 2000 BMW sold Rover and Land Rover, and in 2001 Ford stopped producing the Escort at its Dagenham plant. These changes affect many people and other businesses. For example, the car works at Cowley in Oxford employed over 25 000 workers in the 1970s. By 2000 it employed just 2500 workers. But in 2001 production of the new Mini created more than 1000 extra jobs (photographs **A** and **C**).

Despite these changes, many companies still make cars and commercial vehicles in the UK. As shown on map **D**, many of them are specialist firms. As well as car manufacturers, over 1250 other companies make car components, and more than 100 000 people work in the car components industry, which makes £8 billion a year.

# Changes in car production

More and more new cars are being made and sold. In the UK in 1999:

- new car registrations reached 2.2 million, the fourth highest figure on record

- sales of cars were worth more than £31 billion

- car production reached its highest level since 1972, but the manufacture of vans, lorries and coaches declined.

As well as changes in the number of cars produced, car manufacturers sell increasing numbers of cars abroad as **exports**. More than 1.1 million passenger cars were produced for export in 1999 – more than three times the exports in 1990.

# Changes in investment

When a car company wants to build a new car, it needs to **invest** money in new designs, new equipment, and sometimes new factories. These are very expensive. Since the late 1970s Japanese and American car companies have invested huge sums of money in the European car industry, much of it in the UK. Since 1997, companies have invested over £3 billion in the UK car industry, creating approximately 9700 jobs.

**D** Car production in the UK, 2000

| Number on map | Company | Location | Number of cars produced |
|---|---|---|---|
| 1 | Nissan | Sunderland | 271 157 |
| 2 | Ford | Dagenham | 190 970 |
| 3 | Vauxhall | Luton | 184 243 |
| 4 | Toyota | Burnaston | 178 660 |
| 5 | BMW | Longbridge | 172 099 |
| 6 | Vauxhall | Ellesmere Port | 168 035 |
| 7 | Land Rover (BMW) | Solihull | 166 101 |
| 8 | Peugeot | Coventry | 162 921 |
| 9 | Ford | Halewood | 115 479 |
| 10 | Honda | Swindon | 114 479 |
| 11 | Jaguar/Daimler (Ford) | Coventry | 86 317 |
| 12 | Ford | Southampton | 66 814 |
| 13 | BMW | Cowley | 53 673 |
| 14 | Leyland Trucks | Leyland | 8 115 |
| 15 | Lotus | Norwich | 3 374 |
| 16 | London Taxis International | Coventry | 3 142 |
| 17 | TVR | Blackpool | 1 460 |
| 18 | Rolls Royce/Bentley | Crewe | 1 440 |
| 19 | Metrocab | Tamworth | 624 |
| 20 | Aston Martin | Banbury | 565 |
| 21 | Aston Martin | Newport Pagnell | 57 |

## Activities

1. Study photograph **A**, which shows the BMW's factory at Cowley. Draw a sketch of the site and label the features that help describe and explain its location. Use the list of factors to help you.

2. Use a large copy of map **D** to help you investigate the distribution of the UK car industry.

   **a** Use different colours to highlight:

   - mass-production factories (over 100 000 vehicles)

   - medium-sized factories (10 000 – 100 000 vehicles)

   - small specialist factories (under 10 000 vehicles).

   **b** Use symbols to identify the factories owned by multinational companies.

   **c** Add labels to your map, or write a short paragraph describing the distribution of car factories, then explain your findings.

3. Study the data in map **D** and read the text again. Why is the closure of car factories so important to the local and the national economy?

## Research activity ICT

4. The Internet is a useful way for geographers to collect data. It is easy to find information from a range of sources, including newspapers, governments, companies and pressure groups.

*Remember:* some information on the Internet is unreliable or wrong. It might be biased in favour of the people who produced it.

Visit the website for the statistics section of the UK auto industry using www.heinemann.co.uk/hotlinks.

Search for data on the world's largest vehicle manufacturers.

**a** How many of the world's top ten largest manufacturers belong to the UK?

**b** Which country has the most companies in the world's largest car companies?

**c** What changes in UK car production can you identify?

# Case Study
## Cowley

### Rover fact file

- 🌀 1904: First Rover car produced.
- 🌀 1994: Rover bought by BMW, who paid £800 million.
- 🌀 Brands – Rover, Land Rover, Range Rover, Mini and MG.
- 🌀 Main UK factories at Longbridge, Solihull, Cowley and Swindon.
- 🌀 1999: Employed 37 000 people, with 50 000 jobs at firms supplying Rover.
- 🌀 1999: UK sales ranked sixth behind Ford, Vauxhall, Peugeot, Renault and Volkswagen.
- 🌀 1994–2000: Rover lost £550 million, with sales down 45 per cent.
- 🌀 2000: BMW sold Rover, MG and Land Rover.
- 🌀 2001: Production of the new BMW Mini began at its Cowley factory.

## Back to the future for Cowley

The Cowley factory was closed in 2000 while BMW invested £230 million in new machinery and facilities to produce the 'Car of the Century' – the new Mini – there. For almost a year the workforce was retrained by visiting BMW factories in Germany and USA. Mass production of the new car at Cowley began in April 2001. BMW's plan is to produce 30 000 Minis in 2001, rising to 100 000 a year.

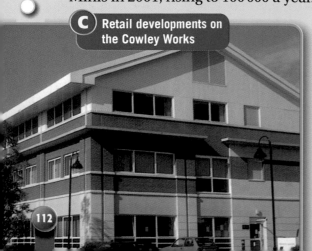

**C** Retail developments on the Cowley Works

## BMW at Cowley

In 2000 BMW sold its Longbridge and Solihull factories but decided to keep the Cowley Works to produce the new Mini there. The Cowley Works is now more **automated** than it was in the 1970s and uses robots rather than people. Employment declined from 25 000 at the factory's peak in the 1970s to 2500 in 2000. Maps **A** and **B** show that even the size of the factory **site** has declined. Land has been sold off for an out-of-town shopping centre (photo **C**), a new business park (photo **D**), and new housing. Because of its good location next to a dual carriageway and on the edge of town, it has proved popular with the developers.

**A** Extract from an OS map of the Cowley Works during its heyday, scale: 1: 25 000

**B** Extract from an OS map of the Cowley Works in 2001, scale 1: 25 000

1960 — The original Mini went on sale in 1959 and cost £496
The Mini was designed as a rival to the German 'bubble car'

1970 —

In the 1970s, at the height of its popularity, the Mini was produced in Belgium, Italy, Spain and Australia

1980 —

The Mini was voted 'Car of the Twentieth Century' by *Autocar* magazine
The last, 5 387 862nd, Mini was driven off the Longbridge production line in 2000

1990 —

2000 —

The new generation of Minis were first produced in Cowley in July 2001 and the cheapest model cost £10 300

**D** This retail park has been built on part of the former Cowley Works

**E** The Cowley Works today

# Activities

**1** Study maps **A** and **B**.

**a** Find map evidence that the Cowley factory has become less important. List the evidence or make a sketch map and add labels around it.

**b** With a partner, discuss the effects of this decline on local people and businesses, and on the local environment. Remember there may be positive as well as negative effects.

**c** Make notes from your discussion using a copy of the table below to help you:

|  | Positive effects | Negative effects |
|---|---|---|
| On people |  |  |
| On businesses |  |  |
| On the environment |  |  |

**d** Write a short paragraph explaining who or what you think are the winners and losers from the changes at Cowley.

**2** Study photograph **D**.

**a** What kinds of businesses would you expect to find in a building like this?

**b** How does the site differ from the Cowley factory (photograph **E**)?

# Research activity ICT

**3** **a** Study an on-line map of the Oxford area from the Oxford City website through www.heinemann.co.uk/hotlinks

**b** Compare the information on this map with maps **A** and **B**. How useful is the on-line map? Give reasons to support your answer.

**c** What map evidence is there to suggest that the location of the site is a good one for developers?

**d** Investigate and compare maps of Oxford from other websites such as Ordnance Survey or Map Blast! at www.heinemann.co.uk/hotlinks

**4** **a** Investigate BMW's UK website using the Heinemann web address to see what you can find out about the Mini.

**b** Click on the icon for Heritage, and find out when BMW was started, by whom, and what the company produced.

**c** Make a timeline for BMW, similar to the timeline above for the Mini.

# Case Study

## BMW – a European and global car manufacturer

**Key**
- Munich Headquarters
- Production
- × Assembly plants
- ○ Sales and distribution locations

**● Production**
Berlin Plant
Birmingham Plant, UK
Dingolfing Plant
Eisenach Plant
Harms Hall Plant, UK
Landshut Plant
Munich Plant
Oxford Plant, UK
Regensburg Plant
Rosslyn Plant, South Africa
Spartanburg Plant, USA
Steyr Plant, Austria
Swindon Plant, UK
Tritec Motors Ltda, Curitiba, Brazil
Wackersdoft Plant

**× Assembly plants**
Toluca Plant, Mexico
Arnata City Plant, Thailand
CKD Production Cairo, Egypt
CKD Production Jakarta, Indonesia
CKD Production Kuala Lumpur, Malaysia
CKD Production Manila, Philippines
CKD Production Kaliningrad, Russia
CKD Production Hanoi, Vietnam

**○ Sales and distribution locations**

| | | |
|---|---|---|
| Argentina | Italy | Sweden |
| Australia | Japan | Switzerland |
| Austria | Mexico | Thailand |
| Belgium | New Zealand | USA |
| Brazil | Netherlands | |
| Canada | Norway | |
| Finland | Philippines | |
| France | Russia | |
| Germany | South Africa | |
| United Kingdom | South Korea | |
| Indonesia | Spain | |

**A** BMW's global activities, 2000

The car industry in Europe is complex and fast-changing. There are many different car manufacturers – most of these have a number of factories, often in different countries. BMW, based in Germany, is one of these multinational companies. Like other car manufacturers:

- Important decisions are taken at the company's **head office** located in a large city. BMW's head office is in Munich.

- Car assembly factories put together large parts of cars which have been made somewhere else. They are often located where wages are low, e.g. in South-East Asia.

- Car production factories make whole cars from start to finish, so they are usually located in areas with a skilled workforce, e.g. BMW has production factories in Germany and Austria.

- Sales offices are often located in cities where there is a big enough market of wealthy people to buy the cars.

**B** BMW's headquarters in Munich

## BMW's success

**C** The production factory in Spartanburg, USA

BMW is a highly successful company, with a reputation for making high-quality cars which are at the forefront of new technology. This image has helped make sure that year after year its sales continue to increase. As an example, in the USA General Motors and Ford sell many more vehicles, but BMW makes more than twice as much profit on each car it sells. BMW is not alone in its success. In Germany as a whole the car industry grew in the 1990s. For example, 75 000 new jobs were created between 1998 and 1999 and over DM700 million (£250 million) was invested in the industry in the years between 1995 and 2000. German car factories make 35 per cent of the total production in the European Union and 14 per cent in the world.

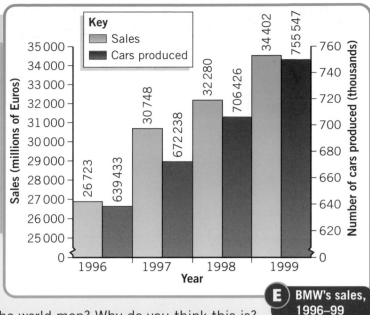

**Key**
- Sales
- Cars produced

Sales (millions of Euros)
- 35 000
- 34 000
- 33 000
- 32 000
- 31 000
- 30 000
- 29 000
- 28 000
- 27 000
- 26 000
- 25 000
- 0

Number of cars produced (thousands)
- 760
- 740
- 720
- 700
- 680
- 660
- 640
- 620
- 0

1996 — 26 723, 639 433
1997 — 30 748, 672 238
1998 — 32 280, 706 426
1999 — 34 402, 755 547

Year

**E** BMW's sales, 1996–99

## Activities

① **a** Copy map **A** and use text boxes to annotate it. These notes should describe and explain the distribution of BMW's activities. (ICT)

**b** Which of BMW's activities do not show up on the world map? Why do you think this is?

② Study the information about BMW.

**a** With a partner, discuss the effects of BMW's success for people and businesses in Munich, and on the local environment. Remember there may be positive as well as negative effects.

**b** Make notes from your discussion using a copy of the table below to help you:

|  | Positive effects | Negative effects |
|---|---|---|
| On people |  |  |
| On businesses |  |  |
| On the environment |  |  |

**c** Write a short paragraph explaining who or what you think are the winners and losers from the changes at BMW.

## Research activity (ICT)

③ **a** Investigate other car manufacturers in Europe by searching the Internet. You could work in groups, with each group investigating a different company.

**b** Find out the image of the company each website presents, and discuss what message it is trying to give to its customers.

**c** Find out what the site tells you about changes in the company.

**d** Compare the geographical information you have found out from each site – for example, where the company's activities are, and whether these are changing.

**help!**

You might like to think about people and places outside Germany too.

④ **Extension**

**a** Investigate BMW's environmental policies using its website through using links in www.heinemann.co.uk/hotlinks. List the measures the company says it is taking to protect the environment.

**b** Find a website for an environmental pressure group, such as Friends of the Earth. Investigate their views on transport issues, and especially the effects of cars. List the key points.

**c** Compare the views of the car manufacturer and environmental groups, explaining any similarities and differences you have found.

# Car production in Europe

**Key**
Car production, 1995 (thousands)

Sweden 388

UK 1 532

Germany 4 360

France 3 050

Spain 1 959

Italy 1 423

**A** Car production in Europe, 1995

The market for cars in western Europe has grown from 13.4 million in 1997 to more than 15 million in 2000. At the same time, the market in North America has been booming. Wealthy consumers there are especially important for specialist European brands such as BMW, Mercedes and Porsche.

In spite of this, the car industry in western Europe is in crisis. A major problem is over-capacity. Car factories here are able to produce over 21 million cars a year, but in fact they sell only about 14.4 million cars a year. One solution is to cut costs by moving production to cheaper locations, for example Eastern Europe, where wages are lower. Another solution is global restructuring to try to cut costs. Many European car manufacturers have taken over, or been taken over by, multinational car companies. For example:

⑥ Ford recently bought Land Rover and gained control of Volvo

⑥ Daimler merged with Chrysler, then secured Mitsubishi.

Of course, these changes often have an impact on people, places and the environment near the car factories, as well as further away. Where there is economic change, there are usually winners and losers.

## Activities

Map **A** shows car production in the mid 1990s. The research activity requires you to update it with current information.

**1** Describe the pattern of car production shown in map **A.**

**2** Suggest reasons why some European countries produce more cars than others.

### Research activity (ICT)

**3** As well as searching for information, geographers can collect information from the Internet and present it in a variety of forms, using word processing or spreadsheets, for example. But good geographers never copy directly – they always select information and adapt it to make it their own work.

**a** Use the Internet to investigate car production in Europe, using one of these websites in www.heinemann.co.uk/hotlinks

⑥ UK Auto Industry statistics page, or

⑥ German Verband de Automobilindustrie.

**b** Find out about changing car production in Europe, using these headings to help you:

⑥ the main car-producing countries

⑥ changes in car production in the past 5–10 years

⑥ the main car-manufacturing companies.

**c** You could present your data by:

⑥ copying information into a spreadsheet, then using the program to sort the data and present it as charts

⑥ selecting useful text, copying it into a word processor, then editing it by using bullets and subheadings, and highlighting key points

⑥ using a presentation program to present your findings and your conclusions about change.

# Review and reflect

## Activities

**1** You are familiar with finding answers to questions, especially geographical questions like the Six Ws: **W**hat? **W**here? **W**ho? **W**hen? **W**hy? Ho**W**? In pairs, look back over this unit and work out suitable questions to go with the answers below.

**a** 58.2 million.

**b** Car components.

**c** Workers and other businesses at Cowley.

**d** Workers and other businesses in Munich.

**e** Mainly in Europe and North America.

**f** Wages are lower there, so companies can make better profits.

**g** General Motors.

**h** A skilled workforce.

**i** It might be biased or unreliable.

**j** Robots do many tasks in the factory.

**help!**

Remember, some questions have only one answer, others can have several answers.

**2 a** Work out between five and ten of your own answers on the theme of the changing car industry. Try to make sure you have at least one for each of the Six Ws.

**b** Test a partner to see if they can work out the questions to go with your answers.

**3** Write a short report on the changing car industry and its effects, using the Six Ws to help you write headings. Use map **A** to help you write about the global car industry. If you use a word processing or presentation program to present your report, you could include hyperlinks to the most useful websites you have used in this unit. (ICT)

**Key**

○ Location
● Finished vehicles
◆ Parts sets
✛ Individual sets
■ CKD (completely knocked down) vehicles, i.e. the unassembled parts of one vehicle shipped together
★ Assemblies
▼ Spare parts

VW Canada
VW America
VW Mexico
VW Brussels — VW AG
Seat
Audi AG
TAS
Autolatina Brazil
Autolatina Argentina
VW Nigeria
VW South Africa
VW Japan
VW Shanghai

N

0   3000 km

**A** VW – a global company

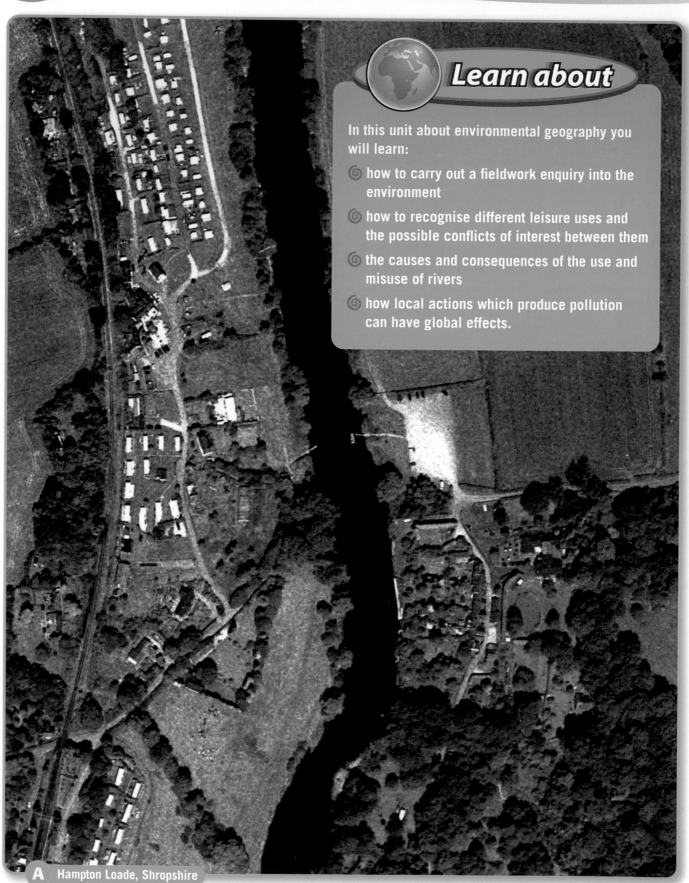

## Learn about

In this unit about environmental geography you will learn:

- how to carry out a fieldwork enquiry into the environment
- how to recognise different leisure uses and the possible conflicts of interest between them
- the causes and consequences of the use and misuse of rivers
- how local actions which produce pollution can have global effects.

**A** Hampton Loade, Shropshire

# Fieldwork enquiry

A class of students were doing some geographical fieldwork by the River Severn. Each student was expected to focus their investigation on one of these questions, although they were encouraged to develop further questions as their fieldwork progressed.

- How has the settlement changed over the years?
- What land use is found on and by this stretch of river?
- How could the tourist industry in the area be expanded?
- What visitor pressures are there on the settlement?
- What conflicts occur as a result of the land use in this area?

The next four pages show how one student went about his enquiry. You will be asked to decide which enquiry question he chose. First of all, Edward got the most detailed map that he could find. He tried the Environment Agency (use the links at www.heinemann.co.uk/hotlinks).

**B** The situation of Hampton Loade, Shropshire

**C** Introducing Edward

**D** OS map of Hampton Loade, scale 1:25 000

# Local actions: profile of a ferryman

The first thing Edward noticed was the last surviving rope ferry on the River Severn. He spoke to the ferryman and took some photos; you can see what he found out on this page.

There has been a passenger ferry at Hampton Loade since the seventeenth century. It was originally used to ferry miners to work on the other side of the river, but it is now used only by tourists. Darren took over the rope ferry in 1996, and relies on hot, sunny weekends in order to make a small profit.

**E** **The rope ferry at Hampton Loade**

**F** **How the rope ferry works**

N
W ← → E
S

River current

Rope across river

LS

**F**
Ferry moves

LS

Rudder

Car park

Key
F   Ferry
LS  Landing stage

I can see that one day I may be forced to give up, and that will be another piece of English heritage lost forever. If the weather is poor, no one visits the area at all. Many of my passengers come by the Severn Valley Railway – there's a beautiful little station 200 metres up the hill. If that's not running, I might as well not bother! People also stay at home if there's a big sporting event on the television. I can't really go away during the summer, because if I don't offer the service, people won't come back. During the winter, however, I have to be very aware of the water level. Last winter's flooding was a nightmare. Both the landing stages that people use to get onto the ferry were destroyed by debris, including uprooted trees, that the flood water brought down from upstream. They can cost £1000 each to replace. If I can't get funds from another source, I feel it's just a matter of time before I go broke!

I live in a small caravan on the western side of the Severn. When a passenger wants to go across the river, they ring a bell and I appear! The ferry is unlocked from its mooring and by moving the rudder I can use the current of the river to move the boat across to the other side.

**G** **Darren the ferryman**

# What leisure activities are located on and by the river?

Edward discovered from a noticeboard that Hampton Loade is a small settlement on the banks of the river Severn in Shropshire. It is now a peaceful riverside scene, but 150 years ago it was very industrial, with mills and forges nearby producing paper, flour and iron.

The settlement has houses on both sides of the river. On the eastern side there is a pub, a restaurant and one or two dwellings. The western side contains more buildings, including a railway station served by the Severn Valley Railway, which often runs steam locomotives.

Edward made field sketch **H** of the settlement during a visit in late August.

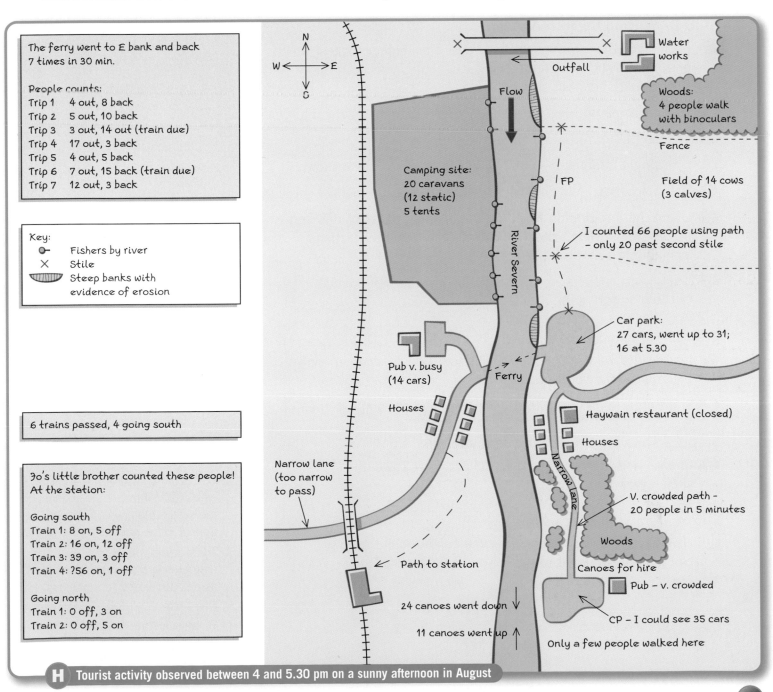

The ferry went to E bank and back 7 times in 30 min.

People counts:
Trip 1   4 out, 8 back
Trip 2   5 out, 10 back
Trip 3   3 out, 14 out (train due)
Trip 4   17 out, 3 back
Trip 5   4 out, 5 back
Trip 6   7 out, 15 back (train due)
Trip 7   12 out, 3 back

Key:
⊶   Fishers by river
✕   Stile
▱   Steep banks with evidence of erosion

6 trains passed, 4 going south

Jo's little brother counted these people! At the station:

Going south
Train 1: 8 on, 5 off
Train 2: 16 on, 12 off
Train 3: 39 on, 3 off
Train 4: ?56 on, 1 off

Going north
Train 1: 0 off, 3 on
Train 2: 0 off, 5 on

N
W ← → E
S

Outfall
Water works

Flow

Woods:
4 people walk with binoculars

Fence

Camping site:
20 caravans
(12 static)
5 tents

FP

Field of 14 cows
(3 calves)

River Severn

I counted 66 people using path – only 20 past second stile

Car park:
27 cars, went up to 31;
16 at 5.30

Pub v. busy
(14 cars)

Ferry

Houses

Haywain restaurant (closed)

Houses

Narrow lane

Narrow lane
(too narrow to pass)

V. crowded path – 20 people in 5 minutes

Woods

Path to station

Canoes for hire

Pub – v. crowded

24 canoes went down ↓

CP – I could see 35 cars

11 canoes went up ↑

Only a few people walked here

**H** Tourist activity observed between 4 and 5.30 pm on a sunny afternoon in August

# Writing up the fieldwork enquiry

Edward was told to write up his field enquiry in four parts:

- Step 1: asking questions – the introduction
- Step 2: collecting information – this section would include primary and secondary data
- Step 3: showing the results – the data is analysed in this section
- Step 4: drawing conclusions – the analysis is used to answer the opening question.

## Activities

### Step 1 – Writing the introduction

**1** Looking at the information that Edward collected, suggest which enquiry question he chose (see page 119).
Give reasons for your answer.

**2** Using OS map **D**, describe the *site* of the settlement Hampton Loade.

**3** Choose the term that best describes the settlement:

  single building   village   sub-town   market town.

**4** Using an atlas, describe the *situation* of the settlement.

**5** Using the information found on the opening pages of this unit, prepare a list which describes briefly the tourist attractions available in Hampton Loade.

**6** Using your answers to activities **1–5**, write the introduction to the fieldwork enquiry.

### Step 2 – Collecting the data

**7** List all the data that Edward collected. Decide whether each piece is *primary* or *secondary* data.

**8** What other data would they have to collect to complete their enquiry?

### Step 3 – Showing the results (data analysis)

**9** Choose and illustrate the data collected by Edward in sketch map **H**.

### Step 4 – Drawing conclusions

**10** Using your answer to **9**, write some conclusions that you can make as a result of the Edward's fieldwork.

**help!**

An introduction should be more than just the enquiry question. Successful introductions contain some background information to 'set the scene' in a geographical way.

**help!**

- Use aerial photograph **A** and OS extract **D** to improve the accuracy of the sketch map, which should appear in the middle of your display.
- Try to use a variety of graphs and diagrams to display the data as well as detailed labels (annotations) and sketches.
- When selecting the data make sure that you link it back to the enquiry question chosen in **1**.

# What conflicts occur between recreational activities?

Geographers sometimes call places like Hampton Loade **honeypot sites**.
Such sites attract great numbers of visitors, especially in the summer season,
at weekends, and during fine weather.

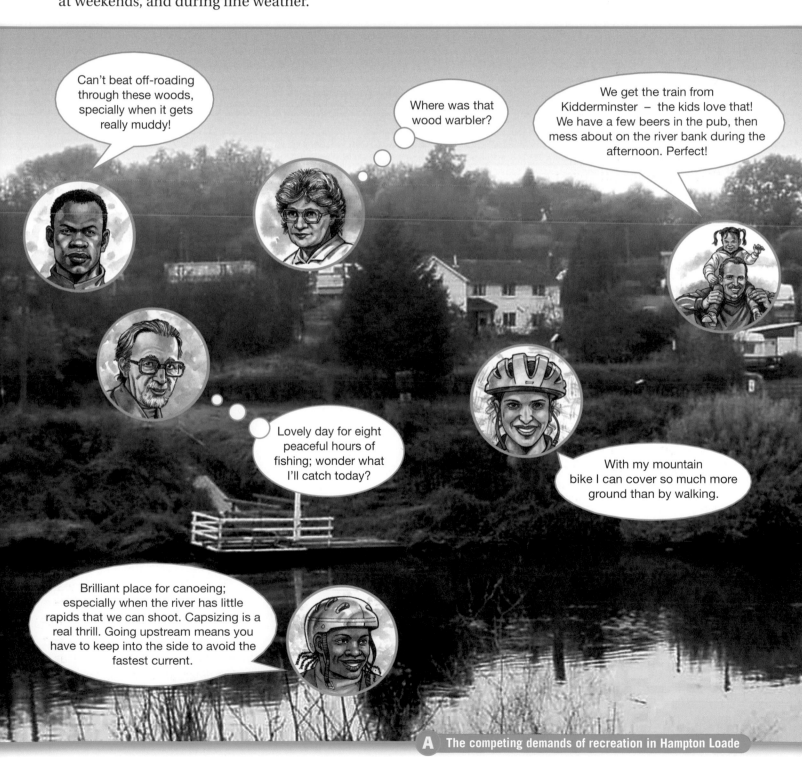

**A** The competing demands of recreation in Hampton Loade

## B Tourism – for and against

### The good points

- Tourism brings money and jobs to areas which otherwise would have little local employment.

- Money from tourism can be used to improve local infrastructure, such as utilities (gas, electricity supply, mains drainage), television reception and mobile phone coverage. Better roads and facilities like shops, public transport and street lighting benefit local people.

### The not-so-good points

- Honeypot sites can get so busy that some regulation is needed. If these areas are not carefully controlled, the things that people come to visit may become spoilt and the area will not be visited anymore.

- The tourist season is very short, especially in Britain where the weather is unreliable, so that many of the jobs only last for part of the year.

- Many of the jobs created by the tourist industry are neither highly skilled nor well paid.

### The conflict

When people visit an area, they usually need a focus for their recreation. For example, the variety of recreational activities on offer at Hampton Loade is excellent for attracting visitors. Unfortunately, there can be some conflict between the activities that visitors choose to do.

## Activities

1.  a  Use the speech bubbles on **A** to make a list of some leisure activities in Hampton Loade.

    b  Add any other leisure uses that you can think of to your list. You may find OS map **D** on page 119, sketch map **H** on page 121 and other information in this unit useful.

2.  Write a short description of the ideal conditions for each of the leisure uses you have listed.

3.  Use your answer to question **2** to help you complete a conflict matrix to show how each leisure activity might conflict with other recreational activities. The matrix has been started for you.

4.  Taking each recreational activity in turn, give reasons for the pattern of conflicts in your matrix.

5.  Because conflict matrices are good at showing which activities cause the most conflicts, planners use them to decide which activities should be most controlled. Based upon your answers to questions **3** and **4**, suggest which recreational activity should be the most controlled in this area.

|  | **Fishing** | **Walking** | **Canoeing** |
|---|---|---|---|
| **Fishing** |  | ✗ |  |
| **Walking** | ✗ |  |  |
| **Canoeing** |  |  |  |

**Key:** ✗ = some conflict
✗✗ = great conflict
0 = no conflict
? = difficult to decide

# Managing leisure activities to reduce conflict

Conflicts may be resolved in a number of ways.

Skateboarding  Mountain Biking

Nature Trail

Hides for birdwatching

🌀 **Power:** Those activities which are more powerful may 'win the day' because they are either not regulated or earn more money. Recreational activity has to put up with it or disappear.

🌀 **Time solutions:** Conflicts can be reduced by allowing recreational users to operate at different times of the day or year.

**Skateboarders banned from park – council plan purpose-built ramps**

🌀 **Buying off:** The losers in a conflict may be given some form of compensation to make up for their loss. For example, they may be given somewhere else to use.

🌀 **Zoning:** Different activities can be given different areas in which to operate, so that conflicts are kept to a minimum.

🌀 **Amelioration** (lessening the bad effects): The activities of the 'winners' in a conflict are controlled so as to minimise their bad effects.

## Activities

**6** Suggest how each of the following decisions might affect the lives of the residents and other leisure users in the Hampton Loade area.

  **a** Allowing loud music to be broadcast from one of the pubs.

  **b** Allowing small power boats on the stretch of river.

  **c** Closing down the public car park.

  **d** Stopping people using the footpaths in the area.

  **e** Replacing cattle with intensive crops.

**7** On the basis of your answers to **6**, put the five decisions in order of the environmental effect they might have. Write brief reasons for your answer.

**8** Choose one of the decisions in **6** and suggest five ways in which the conflict could be resolved.

**9** Produce a labelled sketch map of the area in which you suggest a full management plan to minimise all the potential conflicts.

**help!**

Try to think of the effects that might result from these decisions and how they might affect the activities of other people.

**help!**

Think about how activities could be zoned:

✪ to minimise disruption of the lives of residents

✪ to reduce conflicts with other recreational activities.

# How do people use and misuse rivers?
## Case Study

### Rhine River Basin and fresh water pollution

The River Rhine is one of the world's greatest commercial rivers. It flows through many important countries in the industrial heartland of Europe: from the Swiss mountains the Rhine's course goes past and into the Bodensee. From there its course marks first the Swiss–German border and then the French–German border. It finally flows through Germany and into the Netherlands. The Rhine basin is very densely populated as a result of highly developed industry, trade and agriculture, as well as a dense network of motorways and railways. Demands on the river have therefore been very heavy. Although the Rhine is much cleaner than it used to be, pollution from manufacturing industry, from farming and from sewage remains a major international problem.

**A** **The Rhine Basin**

N

North Sea

Amsterdam
Rotterdam
NETHERLANDS

Rhine-Ruhr industrial region: largest in the catchment

GERMANY

Rhine

Dusseldorf
Ruhr
Cologne
Bonn

Rhine in its lower 'plains' course: intensive agriculture

Lahn

Frankfurt-Mannheim industrial region: major tributaries join Rhine

BELGIUM

Koblenz

Weisbaden • Frankfurt

Main

LUXEMBOURG

Bingen • Mainz

Gorge section: less opportunity for heavy industry

Ludwigshafen

Saar

Karlsrune

Stuttgart

Mosel

Strasbourg • Rhine

Neckar

Rhine 'rift' valley: gentle gradients and wide flood plain suitable for transport and industry

FRANCE

L. Constance (Bodensee)

First major city on Rhine

Basel

Aare

Upper course: Rhine flows through Alps mountain range

0        100 km

Vorderrhein

SWITZERLAND

Hinterrhein

AUSTRIA

**Key**
Areas with high population density

**B** Sources of pollution on the River Rhine

**C** Water quality on the River Rhine

# How does water become polluted?

## Fresh water pollution

**Too many nutrients in the water**

**Blue-green algae** are naturally occurring organisms which feed off nutrients in rivers and lakes. Algae are broken down by organisms further up the food chain and so, under natural conditions, there is a balance. When waste matter from farming, industry or sewage enters a river it causes a big increase in **nutrients** like nitrates and phosphates, which stimulate the growth of algae. These nutrients, together with strong sunlight, give favourable conditions for an **algal bloom** to occur. The algae multiply so fast that a green scum appears on the surface of the water and toxins (poisons) are produced. Toxins are dangerous to fish, livestock and humans. When the algae die they are broken down by bacteria. The bacteria use up the oxygen in the water, killing other water creatures. Nutrient enrichment of this kind is called **eutrophication**.

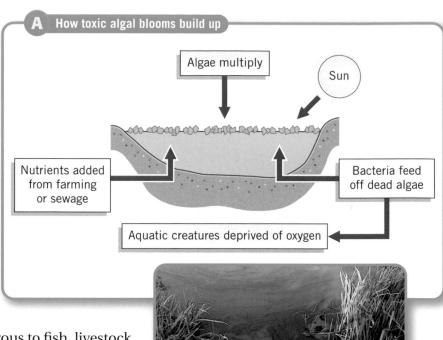

**A** How toxic algal blooms build up

Algae multiply

Sun

Nutrients added from farming or sewage

Bacteria feed off dead algae

Aquatic creatures deprived of oxygen

**B** Green scum appears on the surface of a lake

### The consequences of industrial waste

Factories can discharge heavy metals such as magnesium, zinc and copper into rivers as part of the waste they produce. Rivers **dilute** this waste, but large quantities of heavy metals are toxic. They poison much of the life in both fresh and salt water.

Some chemicals dumped into rivers are not broken down naturally because they are man-made. Many detergents are not **biodegradable** and tiny quantities of these chemicals build up in animals over time. In high concentrations they can kill. This process is called **bioaccumulation**. The situation gets worse when predators at the top of the food chain eat affected animals.

### Rainwater

Falling rain may contain traces of harmful chemicals released into the air by factories and by vehicles. Rainwater that runs off fields which are treated with pesticides or fertilisers, carries the chemicals into rivers. Rain landing on roads can take oil or **particulates** from car exhausts into the drains and eventually into rivers.

**C** Oil and particulates from vehicles drain eventually into rivers

Birds suffer from oil pollution in three ways. It kills their food, and also clogs their feathers so they are no longer waterproof and the birds get cold. When the birds try to clean themselves, they are poisoned by the oil.

D An oiled sea-bird

## Thermal pollution

Factories often use water from rivers for cooling. When the water is returned to the river it is warmer, and this can have environmental impacts. Some bacteria may be killed by just slight increases in temperature. This is called **thermal pollution**.

E A coal-fired power station

### Indicators of pollution

Fish swimming through a river may not be much affected by pollution. But creatures that live on the bed of a river can show pollution levels very well. If conditions are wrong they cannot simply swim away. So these are sometimes called **indicator species**.

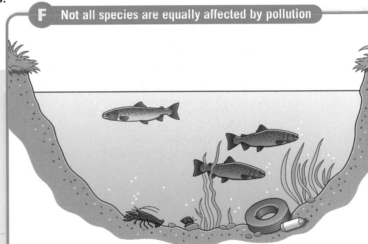

F Not all species are equally affected by pollution

## Activities

1. Make a word bank of key words for this unit. Start with the words in bold on this page. Add any key words you have learned from pages 118–128.

2. Salmon need to travel up river to spawn (lay eggs). They must find a place with good quality, shallow water and a river bed made up of *gravel*, not *silt*. Imagine that you are a salmon making your way up the River Rhine from the sea. Describe your journey, noting any changes in water quality that you come across – try to explain these pollution events. Looking up the international IKSR website through www.heinemann.co.uk/hotlinks might help you. ICT

3. a Take each of the sources of pollution on the River Rhine and explain how they affect the river.

   b Draw a scale of pollution on the River Rhine like the one below. Label the uses of the river onto the scale according to the pollution they cause.

**help!**

Choose from: power station, sewage works downstream of major settlement, intensive agriculture, industry from the Ruhr valley. Your atlas may help you with more.

```
      0    1    2    3    4    5    6    7    8    9    10
      |----|----|----|----|----|----|----|----|----|----|
   Least pollution                              Most pollution
```

   c Explain your answer to **3b**.

4. Using the evidence of changes in water quality from map **C** on page 127, explain how rivers clean themselves as they flow towards the sea.

# 'Behold the sea, the teeming sea ...'

Most river water, and any pollution that it carries, ends up in the sea. The sea has always been used as a dumping ground. In the past people thought the world's oceans were so vast they could absorb any pollution they received. Today some seas are at serious risk from pollution; one example is the North Sea.

## Seawater food chains

**B** There may be many millions of copepods in each cubic metre of water — these graze off the phytoplankton

**A** Plankton are tiny, single-celled plants which float around in the top layer of the sea — they form the heart of the food web

**C** Floating in the sea's currents, jellyfish trap copepods and anything else that swims against their long trailing tentacles

**F** Great grey seals eat a wide variety of fish, crustaceans and sea-urchins

**D** Starfish and sea-urchins feed on a wide variety of shellfish — they are 'keystone' species that control the populations of some other species

**E** Herring and mackerel are surface fish which form shoals for safety from predators

**G** Killer whales feed on large fish, dolphins, seals and even other whales, but they are not known to attack humans

**H** About 90 000 gannets come to the North Sea to breed. They enjoy a diet of larger fish

**I** The wolf fish crushes whelks, scallops, sea-urchins and crabs with its powerful jaws

While the North Sea is one of the world's largest coastal seas, it only contains 1 per cent of the Earth's sea water. It is almost entirely surrounded by land, with the southern part narrowing to a **strait** of water 35 kilometres wide between Dover and Calais. As it is on the **continental shelf**, it is a mainly shallow sea between 25 and 55 metres deep. In the north, the Norwegian Trench is over 200 metres deep.

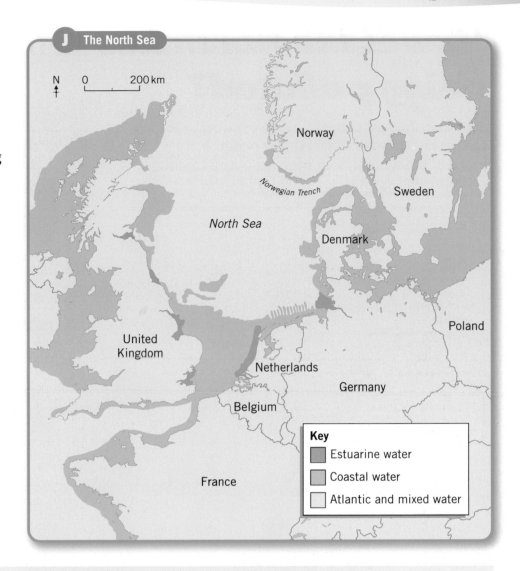

**J** **The North Sea**

N

0     200 km

Norway

Norwegian Trench

Sweden

North Sea

Denmark

Poland

United Kingdom

Netherlands

Germany

Belgium

France

**Key**
- Estuarine water
- Coastal water
- Atlantic and mixed water

## Activities

1. Write a short paragraph to introduce the North Sea. Include information on its location and the scale of the area, as well as an outline of the Sea's physical and human geography.

2. Use the location map and an atlas to list all the distinct environments that exist for wildlife within the North Sea.

3. Using the photographs on the opposite page, construct a food web diagram to show the feeding levels in the North Sea. Start by copying the diagram on the right.

4. **Extension**

   Navigate the website for Ball State University's Exploring Ecosystems at www.heinemann.co.uk/hotlinks to extend your web diagram. (ICT)

5. What factors make the North Sea so at risk from pollution? Extend your writing to compare the pollution potential of the North Sea with that of the Bristol Channel.

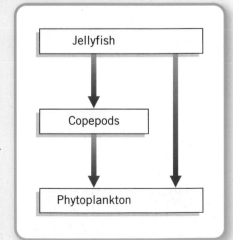

Jellyfish

Copepods

Phytoplankton

# How is the North Sea being polluted?

The Western Margin is important for seabirds and for nursery areas for many young fish species including saithe and herring

The Norway Pout Box protects juvenile stocks of haddock and whiting from industrial fishing for Norway Pout

The North and North-West coast of Scotland is an important spawning area for both cod and haddock

The Wee Bankie area is particularly important for seabirds

**Key**

River-borne nitrogen
- Netherlands 40%
- Germany 22%
- UK 18%
- Norway 7%
- Belgium 5%
- Denmark 5%
- Sweden 3%

Norway 100 75 20 25

Sweden 50 15

Denmark 15

*Norwegian Trench*

North Sea

United Kingdom 430 550 300 265 325 25 15

Belgium 50 80

Luxembourg

Netherlands 650 460 300 280 30 10

Germany 400 250 25 25

France

Poland

Switzerland

**Nutrient levels at sea**
- High
- Medium
- Low

**Key**
- North Sea algal blooms
- Industrial dump site
- Sewage dump site
- Oilfield
- Gasfield
- Pipe
- Saltmarshes

River-borne metals
- Copper
- Chromium
- Lead
- Arsenic
- Nickel
- Cadmium
- Mercury

Values on bar charts are in hundreds of tonnes

0  200 km

**A** Pollution in the North Sea

# Europe's dustbin!

Over 50 million people live close to the shores of the North Sea. It is surrounded by some of the world's most industrialised nations. There is very great stress on the North Sea as it is **exploited** for a number of conflicting uses including:

- intensive use of fish stocks for food
- extraction of water to cool power stations
- extraction of sand and gravel for the building industry
- extraction of natural gas and oil
- as an important shipping route
- as an area for relaxation
- as a huge dump for the unwanted rubbish produced by advanced industrial nations.

The pattern of currents means that it often takes three years for any waste to circulate back into the Atlantic Ocean. The North Sea has become one of the dirtiest and most polluted seas in the world.

## Activities

1. Using map **A**, list all the causes of North Sea pollution. Try to name the country that is the chief polluter for each cause that you list.

2. Try to explain why the Netherlands appears to be adding the most river-borne heavy metals into the North Sea.

3. Explain how the sources of pollution that you have listed could affect each of the creatures mentioned on page 130. Put the creatures in order of danger and explain your decisions.

4. Use map **A** to identify the main areas within the North Sea region which have the most stress from water pollution. You might want to draw a sketch map.

5. Explain at least two effects on the North Sea environment that would result from each of these measures.

   a  An international ban on dumping rubbish at sea.

   b  Using larger tankers to transport oil in the North Sea.

   c  Making companies clean their waste products before they are put into rivers.

   d  Heavy taxes on oil companies who pollute the sea.

   e  Giving each country a strict quota on the amount of fish that can be caught.

   f  Giving extra money to farmers to produce organic food.

6. Suggest any further measures that you think should be introduced to bring pollution in the North Sea under control.

7. Suggest why all progress to clean up the North Sea must be through international agreement. Which nations, in your view, should be involved in making these decisions?

### help!

Ideas could include;

- using satellite imagery
- changing techniques in the fishing industry
- encouraging renewable sources of electricity production
- international co-operation
- controlling air pollution
- building cleaner vehicles.

# Global effects

## Case Study

## What is the future of Antarctica?

### Activities

You are going to use the information on pages 134–139 to conduct a full enquiry using secondary sources. Your enquiry will be divided into the familiar sections:

- **Step 1: asking questions** – some questions have been suggested on this page. Try to break down your main question into smaller questions to help you plan out your work. The introduction should include background information, including the location of the area; you will find suitable material on page 135.

- **Step 2: collecting information** – this section will include secondary data, which you can find on pages 136–139. You can find more secondary information by conducting a web enquiry using a search engine.

- **Step 3: showing the results** – the data is analysed in this section. You will have a great deal of information on Antarctica – pick out only the relevant parts.

- **Step 4: drawing conclusions** – at this point you draw the enquiry to a close by answering the opening enquiry question based upon your analysis.

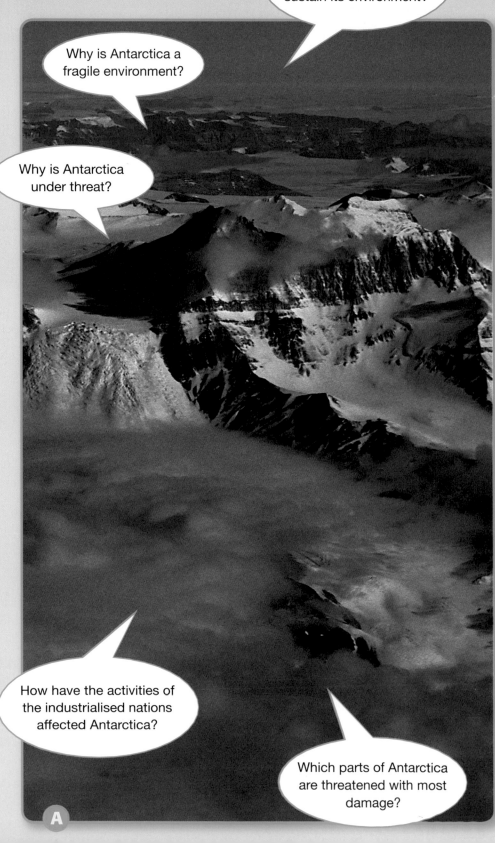

How can Antarctica be conserved and managed to sustain its environment?

Why is Antarctica a fragile environment?

Why is Antarctica under threat?

How have the activities of the industrialised nations affected Antarctica?

Which parts of Antarctica are threatened with most damage?

A

# Antarctica: the last wilderness

The very harsh and difficult environment of Antarctica means that the continent is not threatened by development to the same degree as other places in the world. It is, however, a very fragile environment for a number of reasons.

- Because of the intense cold, the usual processes which cause matter to decay and break down naturally only occur very slowly (see **C**).

- Food webs in this area depend upon one or two key species (see **D**).

- Conditions are so harsh that animals can breed successfully only in one or two areas; these areas are densely populated with animals, which have unique ecosystems.

**ICT idea** More information can be found on websites for Environmental Action and Antarctica at www.heinemann.co.uk/hotlinks

**C** Although this husky has been dead for 85 years, its carcass is preserved by the cold, dry conditions

**B** Antarctica

ATLANTIC OCEAN

0°

Antarctic Peninsula

Ronne Filcher ice shelves

270°

▲ Vinson Massif 5140 m

Lesser Antarctica

Ross Ice Shelf

Greater Antarctica

South Pole

▲ Mt. Markham 4349 m

INDIAN OCEAN

90°

● South Magnetic Pole

Antarctic circle

180°

SOUTHERN OCEAN

0 — 1000 km

**D** Krill form the food for five species of whale, three species of seal, twenty species of fish, three species of squid and numerous birds, including penguins. Krill are fished by mankind and although they are sustainable at present, there are local shortages

# How does global air pollution affect Antarctica?

## The carbon dioxide issue

Greenhouse gases (GHGs) in the atmosphere allow the Sun's rays in but trap radiated heat from the Earth. Carbon dioxide is a gas that occurs naturally and helps to control the Earth's temperature. However, over the past 200 years the burning of fossil fuels has increased the amount of carbon dioxide in the atmosphere. This has led to global warming by the **accelerated greenhouse effect**. A warmer atmosphere is likely to melt parts of the Antarctic ice cap. This could have global effects on sea levels and on ocean currents.

**E** Burning fossil fuels releases $CO_2$ into the atmosphere

## All about methane

Methane ($CH_4$) occurs in much smaller quantities in the atmosphere than carbon dioxide, but is a very powerful GHG. It is produced by rice grown in paddy fields, by cattle, in rubbish tips, and from other sources.

**F** Herds of cattle release $CH_4$ into the atmosphere

## CFCs and the ozone problem

Ozone ($O_3$) is a poisonous substance which causes harmful pollution at ground level. On the other hand, ozone in the stratosphere, 25 kilometres above the Earth's surface, is vital for controlling the amount of incoming ultra-violet radiation. Gases like **chlorofluorocarbons (CFCs)** break down this protective shield. This effect is worse in areas of intense cold, especially in springtime. In most countries CFC production is strictly controlled, but many CFCs will only be released when appliances like old refrigerators are thrown away. The destruction of ozone in the upper atmosphere above Antarctica is one indicator of the effects of this pollution.

**G** False colour satellite image shows ozone 'hole' over the Antarctic

## NO$_x$ and SO$_2$

Sulphur dioxide (SO$_2$) and nitrogen oxides (NO$_x$) are given off by coal-fired power stations and car exhausts. They reach the ground via rainfall or by dry deposition. Their effect is often felt further away as chimney stacks are now built increasingly high. They cause **acid rain**, which not only kills trees but causes streams and lakes to become 'dead' and lifeless.

**H** Pollution from vehicle exhausts can become locked into ice sheets

## Lead and other heavy metals

Lead and other heavy metals are often found in vehicle exhausts and in the smoke released by factories. They can become trapped in the polar ice sheets. In Antarctica there are traces of heavy metals and organic toxins, which have been carried from the inhabited parts of the world. These will be returned to the environment if the ice melts.

**I** Acid rain can kill trees

**J** Dead lakes can look very beautiful but their clear water often means a lack of biological activity

# Is the Antarctic ice sheet getting thinner?

## Massive iceberg peels away from Antarctic ice shelf

A monster iceberg called B-15, 290 km long by 30 km wide, has broken away from Antarctica's Ross Ice Shelf. At 11 000 square kilometres in area, it is about half the size of Wales and looms 50 metres (fifteen storeys) above the water. Although very large icebergs occasionally calve from ice sheets, this one is thought to be the largest one ever.

**K** News report, March 2000

**L** Ice breaking off ice shelf

Cracks in the Antarctic ice shelf have been closely observed since the coming of remote sensing by satellites. The break off of this iceberg is believed to be part of a normal process. Over time, the ice sheet maintains a balance between growth and losses like this.

The recent calving of massive icebergs is a clear sign that global warming is destroying the ice sheets of the western Antarctic. Devastating sea level rises as well as complex changes to the world's climate are now inevitable. Drastic reductions to GHGs are needed now.

**M** Two conflicting views on the Antarctic ice sheet

## The loss of ice shelves from Antarctica

Are the large cracks which have appeared in the ice sheets around Antarctica part of a natural process or an effect of global warming? The *causes* are not certain. Some scientists believe that the *effects* of enormous quantities of ice melting in the Southern Ocean will change our climate. No one today can predict what will happen exactly, but these suggestions have been made:

- The Ross and Ronne ice shelves are like two big plugs which support the ice on the main part of Antarctica. If they melt the whole of the sheet will become unstable.

- The melting of ice shelves, made up of floating ice, will have no effect on world sea levels. However, if lots of cold water is suddenly released into the oceans, this may affect the pattern of ocean currents.

- Ocean currents are important in transferring heat from the Equator to the Poles. They stop the world overheating.

- Most of Antarctica has had a stable climate for the past 40 years. It is only the Antarctic peninsula that is warming at a rate of two to three times the global average.

- If there is less ice on the Poles, then fewer of the Sun's rays will be reflected back into space.

Larsen ice shelf—
Massive loss of ice

Ronne ice shelf—

Ross ice shelf—
together with the
Ronne ice shelf act
as two giant 'plugs'
supporting ice on the
Antarctic landmass

Antarctica

Ronne ice shelf ② Ross ice shelf

Ice

① ← Ice Land Ice → ①

If the Ronne and Ross ice shelves both melt (1), it will be as if two plugs are pulled on the massive layer of ice sitting on top of the land, allowing some of it to slip off (2). Once in the relatively warmer water, melting will be speeded up.

**N** Antarctic meltdown

## Other stresses on the environment

### Mining

Mining in Antarctica has been banned for at least the next 50 years through an international agreement called the Protocol on Environmental Protection to the Antarctic Treaty. There are, however, many valuable deposits of iron, oil and gas. In the future, when these minerals run out in other parts of the world, the pressure for mining here will become very strong.

### Tourism

Increasingly Antarctic cruises are being offered to tourists who are keen to enjoy the wonders of the continent. There are fears that tourists will cause pressure on the fragile vegetation and disturb the breeding grounds of animals.

### Impact of scientists

There are only ever about 10 000 scientists on an area 58 times the size of Britain. All rubbish and waste must be removed from the continent, and it is very expensive to dispose of. In such cold temperatures, the normal natural processes of decomposition are very slow.

O

P

# Review and reflect

## What future is there for the ferryman at Hampton Loade?

**Scenario 1: Business as usual!**

Without agreements between land users, uncontrolled economic development could produce great advantages for a few in the short term. In the long term, it could bring disaster.

**Scenario 2: Stop and think!**

Agreement on stopping global warming might mean unpopular controls, including some on leisure activities. This course of action could provide a better long-term future for all developments.

# Activities

**1** Update your word bank so that it covers the whole unit. This will help you with the final activities. 📖

**2** Read the headlines below. For each headline:

**a** Suggest whether the change is local, regional or global in scale.

**b** Explain what might have caused the change to happen and suggest what effects it might produce.

**c** Suggest how each change would affect the ferryman. Give your reasons.

**help!**

Think of all the possibilities – some might be good but some might be bad.

> **Ozone hole over the Arctic bigger than ever**
>
> **North Sea fishermen forced to catch smaller fish**
>
> **Global temperatures rise and rise!**
>
> **Global warming brings more storms to Britain**
>
> **Cheap fuel for the British motorist: fuel protestors triumphant!**
>
> The Arctic Ocean becomes a major shipping route
>
> **Maldive Islands finally disappear under the Indian Ocean**
>
> **Overharvesting endangers krill supplies**
>
> **European governments agree to control factory emissions**
>
> Breakthrough! Cheap and practical electric car available soon

**3** Look carefully at cartoons **A** and **B**. They show two very different predictions of what might happen in Hampton Loade in the future.

**a** Describe each cartoon and contrast the two predictions.

**b** Try to explain why the two cartoonists have different views of the future.

**c** In your own view, which is the more likely prediction? Give reasons for your viewpoint.

# Glossary

**Accelerated greenhouse effect**  The increased warming of the Earth caused by humans burning fossil fuels. This leads to a build-up of carbon dioxide in the atmosphere, so less heat escapes into space.

**Acid rain**  Rain that contains dilute sulphuric or nitric acid. The acids come from air pollution and are dissolved by the rain as it falls to earth.

**Active zone**  An area where two tectonic plates meet. Earthquakes and volcanoes occur in active zones.

**Automated**  When machines are used instead of people to make things.

**Bioaccumulation**  The process where chemicals build up in the bodies of animals over time.

**Biodegradable**  Able to be broken down naturally and harmlessly, for example by bacteria.

**Blue-green algae**  Algae are small, simple plants that live in water. Blue–green algae increase rapidly in water which is rich in nutrients, especially in strong sunlight.

**Caldera complexes**  A type of volcano which has exploded in the past, forming a large crater. The crater is often filled with a lake or the sea.

**Centralised**  Where power is held by a few people in the capital city.

**Chlorofluorocarbon (CFC)**  A chemical used in some aerosols and fridges which damages the Earth's ozone layer.

**Collision zone**  The area where two continental plates move together and collide.

**Commodities**  Useful things such as cotton, often used for trade.

**Communications**  Roads, railways and other ways of linking people and places, including telephones and computers.

**Communist government**  A government which believes in everyone sharing the country's work and property.

**Components**  The parts that make up something; for example, a car is made up of thousands of different components.

**Consumers**  People who buy goods or services.

**Continental shelf**  The shallow part of the sea around a continent.

**Deep sea trench**  A deep trench or underwater valley formed where continental crust meets oceanic crust.

**Democratic government**  A government which is voted into office by the people.

**Development indicators**  Ways in which development is measured.

**Ecotourism**  Tourism which is in the environment but doesn't damage it.

**Epicentre**  The point on the ground above the focus of an earthquake where the vibration is greatest.

**Eutrophication**  This process can happen in water rich in nutrients. Algae and bacteria grow rapidly and use up all the oxygen, killing other water creatures.

**Exploited**  When a natural resource is used by people.

**Exports**  Goods and services sold by one country to another.

**Factor**  The reason for something, or something which brings about a result.

**Fault**  A break in the rocks caused by movements in the Earth's crust.

**Focus**  The point beneath the Earth's crust where an earthquake starts.

**Fold mountains**  Mountains formed by huge pressures in the Earth's crust which push the rocks upwards.

**Foreshocks**  Small earthquake shocks which come before the main earthquake. They can help warn people of a coming earthquake.

**Greenhouse effect**  A natural process where carbon dioxide in the atmosphere prevents some of the Earth's heat from escaping back into space. It keeps the Earth warm enough to live on.

**Hazard shaking map**  A map to show the areas at risk from earthquakes.

**Head office**  The headquarters of a company, where the company's top bosses work.

**Honeypot site**  Tourist attraction which attracts many visitors, especially during public holidays and the summer months.

**Indicator species**   Creatures which are very sensitive to pollution. If these creatures are found in water they can show the level of pollution there.

**Interdependent**   People or countries who depend on each other.

**Invest**   To put money into a business.

**Kanji**   A type of Japanese writing.

**Lava**   Molten rock which flows onto the surface of the Earth from an erupting volcano.

**Magma**   Molten rock formed deep beneath the surface of the Earth.

**Mainshock**   The biggest shock of an earthquake.

**Manufacturers**   Companies or people who make goods.

**Market**   The place where goods are sold; for example, the main market for Rover cars is in Britain and the rest of Europe.

**Media**   Newspapers, TV and radio altogether.

**Methane ($CH_4$)**   A gas produced by industry, car exhausts and cattle. It is a more powerful greenhouse gas than carbon dioxide.

**Mid oceanic ridge**   A long narrow line of underwater mountains, formed in the centre of an ocean by volcanic activity.

**Monitor**   To check or observe something at regular intervals to see if there are any changes. In earthquake areas, for example, scientists use seismographs to detect the first signs of ground movement.

**Multinational companies**   Large companies which operate in many countries around the world.

**Natural fibres**   Threads or material made from cotton, wool or silk.

**Nutrients**   Food for plants or animals; nutrients are absorbed to help plants and animals survive and grow.

**Open policy**   The Chinese government's decision to open up China to foreign trade and investment.

**Ozone ($O_3$)**   A gas found in the upper layers of the Earth's atmosphere. The ozone layer filters out harmful radiation from the Sun.

**Particulates**   Tiny specks of dust that can form the centre around which raindrops form.

**Perceptions**   How we see or think about something or somebody.

**Plateau**   A large, fairly flat area of highland.

**Prefecture**   A local government area in Japan, similar to a county in Britain

**Site**   The place where a factory or town is built.

**Stereotyping**   Having a fixed idea about what a country or people are like; often a negative idea.

**Strait**   A narrow strip of water between two pieces of land.

**Strato volcano**   A volcano which is made up of layers of lava and ash, built up over many eruptions.

**Sustainable tourism**   Tourism which doesn't damage the environment or people's lifestyles.

**Sweatshop**   A factory where people have to work very long hours, often in difficult or dangerous conditions, for low wages.

**Technopole**   A French centre for science and high-tech industry.

**Tectonic plates**   The Earth's crust is made up of huge slabs called tectonic plates.

**Thermal pollution**   A rise in the temperature of water caused by waste water from factories or power stations.

**Trade surplus**   When a country exports more goods and services than it imports.

**Trade**   Buying, selling or exchanging goods, often between countries.

**Trading partners**   Two or more countries who trade together.

**Transnational Corporations (TNCs)**   Large companies that operate in many countries around the world.

# Index